LITTLE HANDS, BUSY MINDS
DAILY CURRICULUM
FOR TODDLERS AND PRESCHOOLERS
Winter Edition

Jacqueline Salazar De López

Copyright © 2012
Jacqueline Salazar De López

All rights reserved. No part of this publication may be reproduced, stored in a retrieval system, or transmitted in any form or any other means electronic, mechanical, photocopying, recording or otherwise, without the prior written permission of the publisher.

Published by Warren Publishing, Inc.
Huntersville, NC
www.warrenpublishing.net

ISBN: 978-0-9853094-8-0

Library of Congress Control Number: 2012947153

Printed in the United States of America

INTRODUCTION

As a preschool and toddler teacher, I have always strived to develop a daily curriculum for young children that emphasizes language experiences and social interactions, builds upon their interests and fosters development in all areas of development. When we, as educators, demonstrate respect for children's curiosity and listen with open hearts and minds to their comments and questions, we will be able to plan activities that will allow children to discover the world and answer their own questions. When we set up a classroom with a variety of activities, we are giving children the opportunity to explore and learn on their own terms. When we develop hands-on activities, we are empowering children to learn at their own pace. At the same time, we are giving children the opportunity to explore, create, and problem-solve with the materials appropriate for their developmental age.

This book is an account of my field experience and includes activities and ideas I have collected from my children over the years. I hope my personal experiences as a preschool and toddler teacher will help other educators prepare activities that emphasize the process of learning.

In this book, I showcase activities that are suitable for a day, a week or a month but as a teacher, I know that children can center their attention on a topic which differs from what was originally planned. Activities need to be evaluated on a regular basis and the following questions should prompt us to reflect on the continuity or the discontinuity of the topic over a period of time: Are the children interested in the topic? How are the children engaged with the planned activities? Which strategies worked well? Which activities had more participants? What necessary changes had to be made to the environment? When the enthusiasm of an activity exceeds the time frame planed, educators can use the ideas in this book as a foundation for a new project whose length will be determined by the children's interest and engagement. When we do this – that is, adapt our goals in favor of the children's interests – we are swimming into an ocean of opportunities, where the child is the founder, the protagonist of his own experiences and we as teachers, become the co-founders and guides with the responsibility of keeping their ideas afloat. By doing this, we are heading to a new level of teaching experience: a project-based approach. As children take ownership of their ideas, they will make decisions about the direction of their work, expand their knowledge with developmentally appropriate activities and develop a sense of self.

As a teacher, my goal is that this book will be used as a tool and a guide to help teachers plan appropriate activities for children. It is not intended to replace or minimize the planning, observation and documentation of activities done by children which indeed, form the basis of a successful classroom experience.

DEDICATION

This book is dedicated to my family and friends – the source of my inspiration and inner strength to move on and never give up – and to all preschool teachers. I hope the activities and suggestions described in this book will help create an exciting classroom environment that brings out the imagination and creativity of every child. My special thanks to Margaret Dana-Conway from Norwalk Community College who opened my eyes to a world of possibilities while working with little children.

Little Hands, Busy Minds
Daily Curriculum for Two's and Three's

CONTENTS

December..6

January..56

February..106

December

Holidays Around the World

Parent Letter
HAPPY HOLIDAYS!

Dear Parents,

Here we are at the start of a new holiday season. Already children's hearts are filled with joy and excitement! We see streets full of shoppers and homes decorated with lights and ornaments. In this month we will focus on understanding and appreciating different celebrations around the world.

Winter Holidays Around the World is our theme for December. Children will learn songs, finger-plays, poems, and colors and symbols associated with each holiday. We are going to divide this unit into four small segments to help the children acquire a good understanding of:

- Hanukah
- Christmas
- Kwanzaa and Japanese New Year
- Chinese New Year
- Additionally, we will review the color red and the triangle shape.

Some of the holiday activities planned for this month include:

- **Creating holiday decorations**
- **Painting with holiday colors**
- **Identifying shapes and symbols associated with the holidays**
- **Learning holiday rhymes and songs**
- **Playing games with a dreidel (Hanukah) and dominoes (Chinese New Year)**
- **Preparing holiday cookies**
- **Simple hands-on science activities and small experiments such as creating our own play-dough.**

We are looking forward to working on this theme and learning about fun world traditions. Happy holidays to you and your families!

PLANNING WEB
Week #1

Learning Center: SOCIAL - Pair children up and involve them in games that require sharing and taking turns.	**Learning Center: MATH** - <u>Sort the stars</u>: Children can match various colored stars or sort them from largest to smallest.	**Learning Center: LANGUAGE/BOOKS** - <u>Chanukah Lights Everywhere</u> by Michael Rosen - <u>Eight Chanukah Lights</u> by <u>Annie Auerbach</u>	**Group Time** **Small Group:** - Color with crayons on blue and yellow paper **Large Group:** - Play "Hot Potato" game
Learning Center: DRAMATIC PLAY - Set up the dramatic play area with Hanukah-design tablecloths and napkins, plastic foods, utensils, and plates for a holiday meal.	**Developmental Goal:** - Develop an understanding of Hanukah. - Provide children with choices but no more than two or three at a time. **Story/Theme:** - <u>Latkes, Latkes, Good to Eat</u> by Naomi Howland **Diversity:** - Display pictures of children's families and friends celebrating Hanukah		**Routines/Transitions** **Gathering Game:** - Play the "<u>Spin like a Dreidel</u>" game by asking children to gather in a line. Invite children to spin their bodies and move from one area to another.
Learning Center: ART/MUSIC/MOVEMENT - Hanukah handprints - Potato art - "Dreidel, Dreidel, Dreidel" song - "Hot Potato" game	**INDOORS OUTDOORS** <u>Indoors</u>: - Play with Hanukah puzzles <u>Outdoors</u>: - Play "Counting Jumps"	**Health/Nutrition/Cooking** - Wash hands before and after preparing snacks. <u>Snack Idea</u>: - Make potato latkes - Make an edible Menorah	**Learning Center: SCIENCE/SENSORY** - Fill the sensory table with water. Alternate between yellow or blue food coloring each day.

CLASS GOAL

Week #1

HELP THE CHILDREN
IDENTIFY THE COLORS AND SYMBOLS
OF HANUKAH

Day #1

Art Activity

Handprint Menorah: Set out blue and yellow paint. Spread the palm of a child's hand with blue paint and spread yellow paint on the tips of his/her fingers. Let the child press his or her hand firmly on construction paper to make a menorah. Repeat with the other hand, making sure that the thumbs of each handprint overlap.

Circle Time

Start Circle Time by gathering all children in a circle. Read <u>Light the Candles: A Hanukkah-Lift-The Flap</u> by Joan Holub. Ask children to share their favorite part of the story. Write down their responses on chart paper.

Water Play

Fill the sensory table with water. Alternate between yellow or blue food coloring each day. For a better understanding, add a plastic dreidel or menorah to the water table.

Game Play

"Hot Potato" game: Ask the children to sit in a circle. Provide children with a small potato. Play the Wiggles' "Hot Potato". Ask the children to pass the potato around the circle until the music stops. The one holding the potato is out of the circle. Play this game until all players have had a turn.

Music Time

Sit children in a circle. Give each child a plastic dreidel and let him/her spin the dreidel as everyone sings the following song:

I HAVE A LITTLE DREIDEL

I have a little dreidel
I made it out of clay
And when it's dry and ready
Then dreidel I shall play!

Oh dreidel, dreidel, dreidel
I made it out of clay
And when it's dry and ready
Then dreidel I shall play!

Traditional

Writing Center

Provide children with yellow and blue crayons, markers, stencils and paper. Let the children draw, trace and color their designs. If you don't have Hanukah stencils, draw the outline of a dreidel on a piece of cardboard. Cut out the inside of the shape.

Dramatic Play

Set up the dramatic play area with Hanukah-design printed tablecloths and napkins, plastic foods, utensils, and plates for a holiday meal. Invite children to come to the area and encourage them to have a holiday meal. Play holiday music while children are engaged in pretend play.

Day #2

Art Activity

Potato Art: For this activity, gather potatoes, a razor blade (for adult use only), paper plates, paper, and blue and yellow paint. Cut a potato in half. Draw the image of a star on one half of the potato and the image of a dreidel on the other half. Using a razor blade, trace the potato images. Then set out two paper plates and cover them with a sheet of paper towel. Pour blue paint on one plate and yellow paint on the other. Insert a fork as a handle in each potato. Dip the star potato in yellow paint and the dreidel potato in blue paint. Press the paint-covered carved potatoes onto construction paper. When dried, display the artwork around the classroom.

Circle Time

Establish a Circle Time routine. Read <u>Latkes, Latkes, Good to Eat</u> by Naomi Howland. Explain to children that Hanukah latkes are potato pancakes and that they are a staple in every Jewish family. Ask the children if they have ever eaten or helped prepare latkes. If their answer is no, ask them to name the ingredients used in the story to make latkes and go over the preparation. Write their responses on chart paper.

Math Activity

Sort the stars: Cut stars of different colors and sizes (small, medium, and large) out of construction paper. Laminate them. Children can sort the stars by color. Children can also sort the stars from smallest to largest. Another variation of this activity is to tape three laminated stars of different sizes to an empty wall. Add Velcro pieces to each star on the wall. Make sure you have an equal number of small, medium, and large stars. Ask children to sort the stars by size by sticking them to the corresponding star on the wall.

Cooking Idea
Hanukah Latkes:
Gather the children around the table. Assign the children chores like washing the potatoes, cracking the eggs open, and adding the flour and salt. Let every child have a turn mixing the batter. Supervise children in every step and allow them to be part of the process as much as possible.

Ingredients:
- 5 big potatoes
- 3 eggs
- 1/3 cup of flour
- Salt
- Vegetable oil

Preparation:
1. Wash and peel the potatoes.
2. Cook the potatoes with salt and water for ten minutes.
3. Mash the potatoes.
4. Add eggs, flour and salt (if desired). Mix well.
5. Warm up oil in frying pan. Take spoonfuls of batter to fry. Turn latkes over after frying one side.
6. When ready, take out the latkes and let them cool on paper towels.

Puzzle
Hanukah puzzles:
Print Hanukah pictures or take pictures of children playing with dreidels. Mount the pictures on a large piece of construction paper. Make sure to use different backgrounds for each picture (color coded) to help the children sort the pieces by color. Cut the pictures in six or four pieces. Laminate. Let the children sort and play with the puzzles.

Day #3

Art Activity

<u>Hanukah collage:</u> Help children cut small strips of blue and yellow crepe or tissue paper or ask them to tear the paper. Gather pom-poms, yarn, blue and yellow wrapping paper and construction paper. Provide children with blue and yellow construction paper, glue and a brush. Ask children to spread glue on blue construction paper and place yellow materials on top or choose the yellow construction paper and paste the blue materials on top. A variation of this activity is to add yellow paint to the glue and paste blue materials to white paper, and vice versa.

Circle Time

Establish a Circle Time routine. Read <u>Dinosaur on Hanukkah</u> by Diane Levin Rauchwerger. Ask the children to use their imagination and think about what would happen if a dinosaur visited our class. Write their responses on chart paper. Would a visiting dinosaur cause chaos similar to that in the story?

Field Trip
Take the children on a walk to look at the holiday lights on display. Talk about colors and arrangements. Ask children which ones they like best. Do they have similar light decorations at home?

Building with blocks

Children can work together on this project. Help them identify yellow and blue Lego blocks and provide them with bags so they can put away the ones that are of different colors. Give children enough time to sort and store the unneeded blocks. Encourage the children to build different structures using yellow and blue.

Finger Play

Recite and act out the following rhyme with the children.

BRIGHT STAR

Twinkle, twinkle
Bright star
I can see you
From afar
Shining like a light
In the night sky
Please shine on me tonight

Valeria Lopez

Snack Idea

Edible Menorah: Make edible menorahs with the children by following these steps:

1. Provide children with paper plates, bananas, marshmallows, and pretzel sticks. Cut a banana in half and slice it down the middle.
2. Hand out eight pretzel sticks and ask children to stick them into one sliced banana.
3. Count eight marshmallows and press them on top of the pretzels to simulate lit candles. Marshmallows can be previously dipped in yellow food coloring, and dried before use, if desired.

Day #4

Art Activity

Craft Stick Star: Provide children with craft sticks (six for each star), glue, yellow paint, brushes, and glitter. Begin by painting the craft sticks yellow. Paint one side of the stick, allow it to dry, and then paint the other side. Sprinkle glitter. Glue the craft sticks together to form a triangle. Make two triangle sets. Glue an inverted triangle to an upright triangle to form a star.

Circle Time

Establish a Circle Time routine. Read <u>Eight Chanukah Lights</u> by Annie Auerbach. Ask children to help you count the lights as they appear with each turn of the page. Review with children simple words and facts about Hanukah traditions.

Sand Play

Sand Temples: Fill the sensory table with sand. Moisten the sand to help mold it. Provide children with buckets, wheels, shakers, shovels, rolling pins, plastic forks and funnels. Let the children use their imaginations to create sand temples.

Snack Idea

Make blue Jell-O in a tall clear container or use a conventional mold. Follow the recipe on the box. Refrigerate until the Jell-O is firm. This will take up to two hours. When the blue Jell-O is hard enough, add the yellow Jell-O on top. Refrigerate until firm. Unmold the Jell-O so that the children can see the different layers.

Math Activity
Counting Activity Game:

On yellow construction paper, glue blue stars. Make number cards on blue construction paper. Laminate. To play, each child picks a yellow card. They then have to find the blue number card that corresponds to the number of stars.

Science Activity
Sprouting Potatoes:
- Display potatoes on the science table for children to observe.
- Select a potato that may have sprouted.
- To show how a plant seeks sunlight in order to grow, do the following:
    1. Take a small box (or an aluminum tray) and make a 1" round hole on one side.
    2. Place the sprouted potato on the opposite end of the hole.
    3. Put the lid on the box or tray and secure with tape.
    4. Put the box or tray in a sunny spot where the hole will be facing the sunlight directly.
    5. Chart the days until the sprout grows out of the box or tray in search of light.

Day #5

Art Activity

Dreidel Spin Art: Provide each child with paper, a plastic dreidel and paints of different colors. Using an eye dropper, put dabs of paint colors on the paper. Ask the children to spin the dreidel on the paper, allowing all the colors to mix.

Circle Time

Establish a Circle Time routine. Read <u>Where's My Dreidel? A Hanukah Lift-The Flap Story</u> by Betty Schwartz. While reading the story, ask the children to predict where the dreidel could be. Did somebody take it? What can be under each flap? Encourage all children to participate in the discussion and make predictions.

Resource People

Invite a Jewish family member or friend of the class to come in and talk about Hanukah and how it is celebrated.

Show and Tell

Ask children to come to school dressed in blue or yellow or to bring a toy that represents these colors. Encourage children to stand up and share during Friday's show-and-tell.

Finger Play

Ask children to recite the following rhyme. Use a toilet paper tube previously decorated with paint or simple stickers as a pretend candle for children to jump over.

JACK BE NIMBLE

Jack be nimble
Jack be quick
Jack jump over
The candlestick.

Traditional

Game Play

Use the same activity cards from the Math Activity. This activity can be done indoors or outdoors. Ask the children to form a circle. Let a child pick out a number card, identify the number and say it out loud. Then ask all players to jump, turn around, hop, etc. accordingly. Repeat this game until all players have a turn picking out a card.

Writing Center

Cut paper in the shape of a dreidel. Lay out crayons, markers, hole punchers, scissors, scraps of paper, and glue for children. Encourage children to make different designs.

Movement

Play "I Have a Little Dreidel" while children stand in a circle. Ask the children to "spin" from side to side as they sing the song.

PLANNING WEB
Week #2

Learning Center: SOCIAL	Learning Center: MATH	Learning Center: LANGUAGE/BOOKS	Group Time
▪ Discuss family holiday traditions with the children	▪ <u>Bow sorting and counting:</u> Provide children with bows of different colors and sizes for sorting and counting	▪ <u>The Gingerbread Man</u> by Catherine McCafferty ▪ <u>There Was an Old Lady Who Swallowed…</u> by Lucille Colandro	**Small Group:** ▪ Provide white paper and green and red markers for children to draw and color. **Large Group:** ▪ Play "Holiday Hopscotch" game
Learning Center: DRAMATIC PLAY ▪ Create a "Gift Wrapping Center." Supply this area with wrapping paper, colored tissue paper, bows, ribbons, glue, empty boxes, etc.	**Developmental Goal:** ▪ Promote free movement (in a safe area) as a means of self-expression in the classroom. Include dancing with a scarf, running, hopping, etc. **Story/Theme:** ▪ <u>A Wish To Be a Christmas Tree</u> by Michael G. Monroe **Diversity:** ▪ Listen to holiday songs from abroad. ▪ Display pictures of children and their families during the holidays, eating traditional food, home decorations, etc.		**Routines/Transitions** **Gathering Game:** ▪ Laminate photos of each child and place them inside a box with a lid. Pick a child to lift up the lid and take out a picture of another child, who will then pick the activity of his or her choice
Learning Center: ART/MUSIC/MOVEMENT ▪ Holiday collage ▪ Easel painting with green and red ▪ Singing Holiday Songs ▪ "Freeze" dance movement	**INDOORS OUTDOORS** <u>Indoors</u>: ▪ Sorting holiday cards <u>Outdoors</u>: ▪ Play "Ring Around the Presents…."	**Health/Nutrition/Cooking** ▪ Wash hands before eating snacks and meals <u>Snack Idea</u>: ▪ Make green and red Jell-O.	**Learning Center: SCIENCE/SENSORY** ▪ Create a "Mystery Box" with holiday items inside ▪ Add scents and glitter to play-dough

CLASS GOAL

Week #2

HELP THE CHILDREN
IDENTIFY THE COLORS AND SYMBOLS
OF CHRISTMAS

Day #1

Art Activity

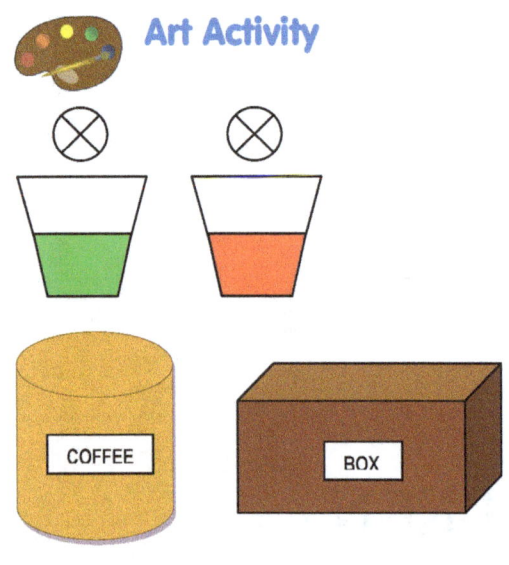

Holiday Marble Painting: Set up the art table with white paper, a large empty box or large coffee can, red and green paint, marbles (use golf balls for younger children), gold and silver glitter, and plastic spoons and cups. Pour paint into separate cups and place spoons and marbles in each cup. Lay paper on the bottom of the box and use a spoon to take a marble from the paint and drop it on the paper. Shake the box or the can back and forth. Continue for as long as the child would like. Take the paper out and sprinkle glitter over the wet paint.

Circle Time

Establish a Circle Time routine. Read The Gingerbread Man by Catherine McCafferty. After reading the book, start the discussion by asking children to retell the events of the story. They can name the characters and recall their actions in the story or simply describe their favorite part of the story. Write their responses on chart paper.

Science Activity

This activity can be done at Circle Time. Trace and cut out a gingerbread man silhouette from sandpaper. Provide children with a cinnamon stick and encourage them to rub the stick on the paper. Let children sniff the scent.

Dramatic Play

Create a "Gift Wrapping Center." Supply this area with wrapping paper, colored tissue paper, bows, ribbons, glue (use tape for older children), empty boxes, etc. Help the children wrap the boxes and decorate with bows or ribbons.

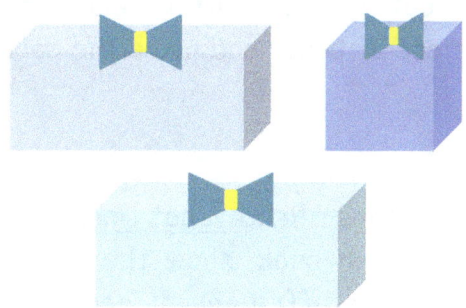

Writing Center

Provide markers, crayons, pom-poms, glue, stamps, stickers, and sandpaper cutouts of the gingerbread man. Encourage the children to draw on and decorate their cutouts.

Movement

Freeze Dance: Play holiday songs on a CD player or a computer. Instruct the children to dance or sing along until the music stops. Then they should freeze and move when music starts again.

Snack Idea

Holiday Wreath Jell-O Mold: Use a Jell-O or baking mold for this activity. Make green and red Jell-O separately following the box instructions and pour one mix into the mold. Place the mold in the refrigerator for fifteen minutes or until it becomes hard. Add the second Jell-O mix on top and refrigerate until it sets. Place cherries or pineapple chunks around the Jell-O wreath. Serve this colorful, edible wreath as a snack.

Day #2

Art Activity
Holiday Collage: Provide children with construction paper, tissue paper, wrapping paper, glue, pom-poms, glitter, pictures of holiday items from magazines, and paintbrushes. Ask children to cut (if they can) or tear paper with their fingers. Let children spread the glue on a piece of paper and place the collage materials on top.

Circle Time
Establish a Circle Time routine. Read <u>What Dogs Want For Christmas</u> by Kandy Radzinski. After reading the book, show the children a wrapped box with a mystery gift inside (it can be a toy, stuffed animal, etc). Pass the box around and ask the children to "guess" what is inside the box. Write their responses on chart paper.

Sensory Play
Use red and green play-dough and holiday cookie cutters to make play-dough cookies. Add glitter and scent (peppermint, pine, etc.) to the dough for children to roll and mix.

Water Play
Add water toys, cups, plastic toys, green or red food coloring to the water table. Also, add items that float or sink in the water.

Math Activity
Color Hunt: Ask children to walk around the classroom to look for items that are red or green. Put all the items together and encourage children to sort and count the items by color and size.

Music Time

Ring Around The Presents: This activity can be played in an open space indoors or outdoors. Gather all children in a circle holding hands. Encourage children to sing Ring Around the Presents.

RING AROUND THE PRESENTS
To the tune of "Ring Around the Rosie..."

Ring around the presents
Red, green expenses
Glitter. Glitter.
We all <u>fall down</u>!

Jacqueline Lopez

Substitute *fall down* for *jump up, twist, clap our hands, dance...etc.*

Building with blocks

For this activity, print out small outlines of candy canes, toys or other related holiday items or use holiday stickers. Glue the cutouts or put stickers on blocks of different lengths. Cover the designs with clear tape. Use these blocks to teach children small to large relationships and number proportions.

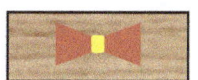 

Field Trip

Take a walk around the school and look for holiday decorations. Ask children to describe what they see.

Day #3

Art Activity

Easel Painting: Set up the easel with paper and red and green paint trays. Let children dip their hands in the paint and place them on the paper in any way they would like.

Circle Time

Establish a Circle Time routine. Read <u>A Wish To Be a Christmas Tree</u> by Michael G. Monroe. After reading the book, ask children to "make a list" of things they want. Ask them to tear or cut out pictures of toys from a toy catalog and glue them to a piece of paper.

Finger Play

Recite this rhyme. Have the children repeat the rhyme with hand movements.

LITTLE JACK HORNER

Little Jack Horner sat in the corner
Eating his Christmas pie,
He put in his thumb and pulled out a plum
And said "What a good boy am I!"

Traditional

Sand Play

Add sand to the sand table. Pour enough water so that the sand can be easily molded into shapes. Provide children with shovels, buckets, holiday cookie cutters, cups and other items for children to play.

Game Play

Jingle, Jingle, Bells Game: Sit children in a circle. Pick a child to be "It." Let the child (It) walk outside the circle tapping each child on the head while saying, "Jingle." Similar to Duck, Duck, Goose, the child who is "It" will tap and choose a child to be the "Bell." The "Bell" child stands up and chases "It." If "Bell" doesn't reach "It" before "It" sits in the empty seat, then "Bell" becomes the new "It."

Puzzle

Number Puzzle Activity: Make puzzle cards to teach children numbers and their correspondents. Fold a strip of construction paper in half. Write a number on one half and glue a picture of a holiday item on the other half. Laminate. Cut the strip into a puzzle shape. Encourage children to count the items and look for the matching picture. To make this activity easier for younger children, make the number cards color coded.

Sensory Play

Feely box: Use a feely box (or mystery box) for this activity or make your own. Draw and cut out a large circle from an empty sealed cardboard box. Ask children to pick three or four small toys that can fit through the hole and drop them inside the box. Ask a child to put one hand inside the box, touch and feel the item and guess what it could be. Encourage children to use descriptive words such as round, little, etc., to describe the object. Continue the game until all players have a turn.

Day #4

Art Activity

Bubble Printing: Set up the art table with a baking sheet, white paint, clear liquid dish detergent, red and green food coloring, drinking straws, white construction paper and a pitcher of water. Mix together a squirt of paint, one or two drops of green food coloring and one spoonful of dish detergent. Add some water until the brew is ready for blowing bubbles. With a drinking straw, ask children to blow bubbles until the tray overflows. Gently place the construction paper on top of the bubbles. Wait for the bubbles to pop and then remove the paper. Repeat the same procedure using red food coloring.

Circle Time

Establish a Circle Time routine. Read <u>There Was an Old Lady Who Swallowed a Bell</u> by Lucille Colandro. After reading the book, ask children to name all holiday items the old lady swallowed. Write their responses on chart paper.

Cooking Idea

Sugar cookies: Buy sugar cookie mix and follow the instructions on the box. Provide frosting and holiday sprinkles for children to decorate their own cookies.

 **Finger Play**

 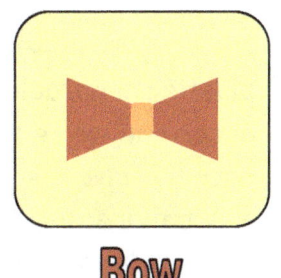 

Bell **Bow** **Gift**

Make copies of <u>There Was an Old Lady Who Swallowed a Bell...</u> Cut out pictures of items she ate. Laminate. Attach a Velcro piece to the back. Using a flannel story board, allow children to repeat the story using the flannel pieces.

Math Activity

Noodle Patterns: Make pattern cards by putting red and green stickers on a pre-drawn chart or gluing red and green construction paper circles to the chart. Laminate. Use red and green Unifix blocks to continue the pattern.

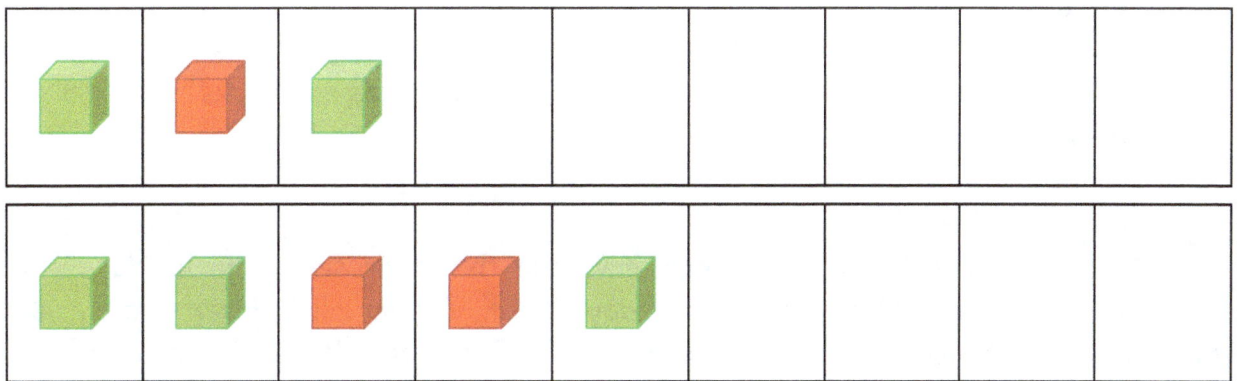

Day #5

Art Activity

Plastic Cookie Receptacle Printing: Set out a plastic receptacle from a cookie tin, bowls of red, green and white finger-paint, and construction paper. Tape the plastic receptacle to the table. Ask children to cover the receptacle with spoons of paint, and to use their fingers to spread the paint. Then, place construction paper on top and press hard to make a print.

Circle Time

Establish a Circle Time routine. Read <u>Bear Stays Up for Christmas</u> by Karma Wilson. After reading the book, ask children what they do with family and friends to prepare for the holidays. Write their responses on chart paper.

Science Activity

Add a collection of different items to the science table for children to explore and see. Add magnifying glasses, evergreen branches and plastic tongs for children to grab and hold needles for observation; add pinecones and books that display pictures of evergreen trees.

Show and Tell

Ask children to bring in to school any item that represents the holidays – a picture, a toy or they can wear holiday colors. Gather all children in a circle. Allow every child to stand up and show his/her item. Encourage the child to describe it. Continue until all children have a turn. Write the names of the items shown on a chart.

Music Time

This activity can be done indoors or outdoors. Gather all children in a circle to sing and act out the following song:

WE WISH YOU A MERRY CHRISTMAS

We wish you a Merry Christmas
We wish you a Merry Christmas
We wish you a Merry Christmas
 And a Happy New Year.

Let's all do a little clapping,
Let's all do a little clapping,
Let's all do a little clapping,
To spread Christmas cheer!

Traditional

Additional verses: Substitute *clapping* for *jumping, marching, dancing, hopping, galloping, turning around* and so forth...

Resource People

Invite a parent or any family member or friend of the class to come and read a holiday story, play holiday songs on an instrument (guitar, piano, etc.) or sing holiday songs.

Art Activity 2

Cut out the front of a holiday card and glue it to a piece of construction paper. Laminate and punch holes around all edges. Provide children with thread. The children can practice lacing the cards.

PLANNING WEB
Week #3

Learning Center: SOCIAL - Review the similarities and differences of each holiday celebration	**Learning Center: MATH** - <u>Ears of corn matching game</u>: Provide matching cards for children to sort and match	**Learning Center: LANGUAGE/BOOKS** - <u>My First Kwanzaa Book</u> by Deborah Chocolate. - <u>A Kwanzaa Celebration Pop-Up Book</u> by Nancy Williams	**Group Time** <u>Small Group</u>: - Make "Unity Cups" at the writing center. <u>Large Group</u>: - Act out holiday songs
Learning Center: DRAMATIC PLAY - Provide props for holiday pretend play: dress-up clothes, dolls, small animal figures, pictures of family celebrations, etc.	**Developmental Goal** - Develop self-control strategies to help children control their behavior. - Promote children's exploration and experimentation with cause and effect. **Story/Theme:** - <u>Japanese Celebrations</u> by Betty Reynolds **Diversity:** - Display pictures of our class family holidays		**Routines/Transitions** - Provide dressing boards to help children master different skills: lace, tie, snap, button, buckle and zip
Learning Center: ART/MUSIC/MOVEMENT - Holiday collage - Kwanzaa flag - Reciting ""Umoja." - Singing "Umoja means unity." - Making a Windsock	**INDOORS OUTDOORS** <u>Indoors</u>: - Decorate origami paper. <u>Outdoors</u>: - Streamers Parade	**Health/Nutrition/Cooking** <u>Snack Idea</u>: - Wash, cook and serve corn for snack	**Learning Center: SCIENCE/SENSORY** - Make play-dough. - Dying noodles.

CLASS GOAL

Week #3

HELP THE CHILDREN
IDENTIFY THE COLORS AND SYMBOLS
OF KWANZAA AND THE JAPANESE
CELEBRATION

Day #1

 **Art Activity**

Kwanzaa Flag: Set out trays with red, green and black paint, rolling pins with designs, tape and paper. Tape the paper to the table. Let children roll the rolling pin on a paint tray and then roll it on the paper. Continue rolling from edge to edge to make flag stripes using different color paints and rolling pins.

Circle Time

Establish a Circle Time routine. Read <u>A Kwanzaa Celebration Pop-Up Book</u> by Nancy Williams. After reading the book, ask children questions about the story. Observe if they can distinguish between celebrations. As a hint, create a holiday wall of art projects that are characteristic of each holiday for children to see and compare. Write their responses on chart paper.

Math Activity

Matching cards: Prepare fifteen ears of corn (traditionally eaten during Kwanzaa). Create one set of five number cards with pictures of ears of corn. For example, the "1" card will have one ear of corn, the "2" card will have two ears of corn and so on. If possible, color-code the cards to help the children sort and match the ears of corn. For example, the "2" card can have two ears of corn on an orange background while the "5" card can have five ears of corn on a blue background.

Finger Play

Recite the following rhyme with the children.

KWANZAA

Kwanzaa, Kwanzaa is here today!
Greet your friends,
Clap your hands.
Turn around,
Hold hands in a circle.
Let's celebrate today
Umoja means unity
(*Hold and raise hands up together*)
For you and me!

Valeria Lopez

Writing Center

Make note pads for the children to write, draw and color by looping together sheets of red, brown and black construction paper cut in half. Provide children with dot-paints, crayons, markers, stickers, glitter, scraps of paper and glue.

Science Activity

Dying noodles: For this activity, you will need uncooked ziti, wagon wheel or any other type of noodle with holes in the middle for stringing. Divide the noodles in three batches and add red, green or black food coloring to each batch. Let them dry on a sheet of paper towel. Move the noodles from time to time so they don't stick to the paper. Replace the paper towel when wet so the noodles don't stick to the paper towel.

Day #2

Art Activity

Kwanzaa Necklace: Provide children with a string and red, green, and black noodles. If children want to personalize their necklace, they can use magic markers to make gentle drawings on their colored dried noodles. Make a double knot on one end or wrap it with a little piece of masking tape to keep the noodles from sliding off. Encourage children to string the noodles in patterns – two wheels and one ziti or three ziti and one wheel and so forth.

Circle Time

Establish a Circle Time routine. Read Lil' Rabbit's Kwanzaa by Donna L. Washington. After reading the book, invite children to recall all the adventures of Lil' Rabbit. Who did she meet first? Write their responses on chart paper.

Writing Center

Kwanzaa window decorations: Make a window decoration for the class. To do this, set up the table with red, black, green and yellow crepe paper streamers and pre-cut letter-sized sheets of contact paper. Tape the contact paper to the table, leaving the sticky side up. Let children tear the streamers and lay them on the paper. When done, lift the contact paper and place it on a window. A variation of this activity is to place the decorated contact paper on a colorful sheet of construction paper to make a placemat called mkeka in Swahili.

Cooking Idea

Boiling ears of corn: Help children wash the corn and place it in a pot. Let children pour water in the pot. Bring water to a rapid boil (five to seven minutes). Cool and serve for snack. To add flavor, add one to two tablespoons of sugar and $\frac{1}{4}$ of milk (if there is no milk allergy) to the boiling water.

Game Play

Tic Tac Toe Safari: Make a tic-tac-toe chart. Laminate. Use red, yellow, and black backgrounds to make animal playing cards. Laminate the cards and glue a magnetic strip to the back of each card. Make sure the cards are about the size of a tic-tac-toe square. Play this game over a magnetic board. Choose two players and distribute six cards of one animal to each of them; that is, one player may have six elephant cards while the second player may have six giraffe cards. Let one player go first by placing his/her animal card on any section of the grid. Then have the other player go next. Alternate until one player has three animal cards in a row (horizontally or vertically).

Music Time

Sing this song during Circle Time.

UMOJA MEANS UNITY

Sung to the tune of: "The More We Get Together"

Umoja means unity, unity, unity.
Umoja means unity for you and me!
Because your friends are my friends,
And my friends are your friends.
Umoja means unity, unity, unity.
Umoja means unity for you and me!

Valeria Lopez

Day #3

Art Activity

Kwanzaa Unity Cup: Provide children with small foam cups; yellow, green and red markers; craft sticks and black paint. Take pictures of two children holding hands and print them out in 5" x 5" size. Laminate. Paint the cup black inside and out. Let it dry. Meanwhile, ask children to color the craft sticks with markers. Glue the pictures on one end of the stick. Insert the stick into the bottom of the cup. Let children lift their "unity" pictures up and down.

Circle Time
Establish a Circle Time routine. Read <u>My First Kwanzaa Book</u> by Deborah Chocolate. After reading the book, ask children to name some of the Kwanzaa symbols or list Kwanzaa class activities. Write their responses on chart paper.

Sensory Play
Gak play: Set up the sensory table with plastic spoons, cups and other kitchen gadgets. Measure four cups of cornstarch and pour in to the table. Add one to two drops of red, yellow and green food coloring from different sides of the table. Add gradually one cup of water. Stir. Let children use their hands and tools to play with the Gak mixture while the colors mix together.

Dramatic Play

Set up the dramatic play area as a Safari place by placing pictures of wild animals on the wall. Mention some characteristics of each animal such as what they do, what they eat, where they sleep, etc. Encourage children to pretend to be each animal by imitating their actions.

Building with blocks

Provide children with blocks. Add small plastic animals to the area. Invite children to build the animals' homes using different color blocks. As a variation of the activity, children can build with blocks at the water table.

Movement

Pass the cup: This game is similar to Hot Potato. Sit everyone in a circle. Have the children pass a plastic cup around while music is playing. When the music stops, the child who has the cup on his hands will stand up, jump, clap, skip, etc. until the music resumes. Continue until all players have a turn.

Sensory Play

Provide children with play-dough and craft sticks. Let children make play-dough balls and attach a craft stick to the dough. Children will repeat the last step until they have seven candles (Kinera).

Resource People

Invite a family member or class friend to talk about Kwanzaa and its implications.

Day #4

Art Activity

<u>Origami Paper:</u> Provide children with sheets of pastel tissue paper, gift wrapping paper, wax paper, paint brush and decoupage solution (*sold at craft stores or easily made by mixing in a bowl three cups of Elmer's glue and one cup of cold water*); q-tips and a small tray of black paint. Help children tear paper in small irregular pieces. Brush a coat of the decoupage solution over wax paper. Place overlapping pieces of tissue paper on the wax paper. Brush a final coat of the decoupage solution over the tissue paper. Let it dry. Dip the q-tip in black paint and let children paint lines across the paper simulating ancient Japanese art.

Circle Time

Establish a Circle Time routine. Read <u>Yoko's Show and Tell</u> by Rosemary Wells. After reading the book, ask children to recall their favorite parts of the story. Write their responses on chart paper.

Sensory Play

Set up the science table with picture books of the Japanese crane, bird seeds, plastic eggs, and a fake nest. Use pictures of the different stages of the Japanese crane for children to compare and contrast their similarities and differences.

Dramatic Play

Set up for a tea party. Remove all chairs. Have children sit on the floor in a kneeling position. Introduce chopsticks and explain to children that not everyone eats with forks or spoons. Pass around paper plates, plastic food and chopsticks. Encourage children to use the chopsticks to pick up the pretend food. Allow children enough time to practice this skill.

Math Activity

Sequence cards: Print out pictures of the Japanese crane (*symbol of long life and good luck*) birth cycle. Cut them out. Laminate. Encourage children to arrange the pieces in the correct order. To help children do this, mount on the wall or tape to the table the correct sequence.

Finger Play

Here's a traditional rhyme that children in Japan recite. If possible, ask a Japanese person to recite it as well.

むすんで　ひらいて
手を打って　むすんで
またひらいて　手をうって
その手を　上に
むすんで　ひらいて
手を打って　むすんで

CLOSE HANDS, OPEN HANDS

Close hands, open hands,
Close hands, open hands

Open hands again, clap hands
Put those hands up.

Close hands, open hands,
Clap hands, close hands.

Traditional

Day #5

Art Activity

Japanese Windsock: Provide children with construction paper, tissue paper, aluminum foil, crayons and markers. Allow children to choose their favorite color of construction paper and draw, color, add stickers, or glue pieces of aluminum foil. Roll the paper up to form a tube and then tape or glue the ends. Cut tissue paper in long strips and let children glue them around the windsock. Punch two holes and tie a string to hang the windsock from the ceiling.

Circle Time

Establish a Circle Time routine. Read <u>Japanese Celebrations</u> by Betty Reynolds. After reading the book, pass a Japanese doll around or show pictures of Japanese dolls and ask children if these outfits are similar to the outfits worn in the story. Children can also simply mention their favorite part in the story. Write their responses on chart paper.

Water Play

Set up the water table. Add pipes, funnels, cups, and eye droppers. Ask the children to pour water through these items. Observe how water flows out of these items. Ask children to compare and contrast the similarities and differences.

Writing Center

Set up the writing center with origami paper, stickers, crayons and markers. Let children draw and color or decorate the paper as they wish.

Sensory Play

Provide children with chopsticks and play-dough (*or make your* own). Encourage children to make designs on the dough using the chopsticks. Add copies of Japanese symbols for children to try to print on the dough with the chopsticks.

PLAY-DOUGH RECIPE

Ingredients:
- 2 cups of flour
- 1 cup of salt
- 2 tablespoons of tartar cream
- 2 cups of water
- 1 tablespoon of mineral oil
- Green food coloring *(The Japanese decorate their stores and homes with greens).*

Preparation:
Mix all ingredients in a saucepan. Cook over medium heat, stirring until a ball forms. Allow to cool, and then knead. Store in a Ziploc bag. Play-dough will last a long time.

Game Play

Bean Throwing Game: Bean throwing in Japan drives away bad luck and invites happiness into homes. To play this game, select large plastic containers and beans (*because beans are small, supervise children at play*). Place the beans in a container and give the same amount to each player. Invite two players to stand two feet from the table and to throw the beans in the containers. Count aloud the number of beans each player successfully throws in the container. The winner of the game is the child that successfully threw the most number of beans in the container. Allow all children to have a turn and encourage them to count the beans out loud to help with number skills and number recognition.

PLANNING WEB
Week #4

Learning Center: SOCIAL - Invite a Chinese person to speak to the children about Chinese New Year	**Learning Center: MATH** - <u>Domino card game</u>: Make domino cards for children to learn colors and numbers	**Learning Center: LANGUAGE/BOOKS** - <u>Dragon Dance: A Chinese New Year</u> by <u>Joan Holub</u> - <u>Lanterns and Firecrackers</u> by <u>Johnny Zucker</u>	**Group Time** <u>Small Group</u>: - Make a paper kite at the writing center <u>Large Group</u>: - Sing and act out finger-plays
Learning Center: DRAMATIC PLAY - Set up the dramatic play area with dusters, brooms, dust pans for children to clean and sweep this area	**Developmental Goal:** - Help children engage in individual or group play. Add new elements to their play area to extend their experience **Story/Theme:** - <u>My First Chinese Year</u> by Karen Katz **Diversity:** - Display real pictures from magazines of Chinese New Year celebrations		**Routines/Transitions** - Turn the lights off in a room to let children know what comes next (*go to sleep, for instance*), or to indicate the noise level is high
Learning Center: ART/MUSIC/MOVEMENT - Fireworks - Painting with watercolors - Lantern craft - "This is the way…" song	**INDOORS OUTDOORS** <u>Indoors</u>: - Play "Chinese CD" for children to dance <u>Outdoors</u>: - Dragon Parade	**Health/Nutrition/Cooking** <u>Snack Idea</u>: - Serve slices of oranges and tangerines for snack - Serve red foods such as strawberries and cherry tomatoes	**Learning Center: SCIENCE/SENSORY** - Fill the sensory table with rice

CLASS GOAL

Week #4

HELP CHILDREN IDENTIFY THE SYMBOLS OF CHINESE NEW YEAR, THE COLOR RED AND THE TRIANGLE SHAPE

Day #1

Art Activity

Painting with watercolors: Provide children with watercolors, paint brushes, paper plates (or watercolor paper), and cups with water. Let children dip the brush in the water cup. Shake the excess water off the brush and sweep it onto the watercolors and then on the paper/paper plate. For better results, add one or two drops of water to each watercolor tray and brush it over the plate/paper. A variation of this activity is to replace the paint brushes for sponges, cotton balls, or q-tips for different effects.

Circle Time

Establish a Circle Time routine. Read <u>Dragon Dance: A Chinese New Year</u> by Joan Holub. After reading the book, ask children to describe Chinese New Year rituals and traditions, or simply recall their favorite part of the story. See if they can compare and contrast Chinese New Year and other holidays studied in previous weeks. Write their responses on chart paper.

Snack Idea

Help children wash the oranges and tangerines. Cut them for snack. Use this opportunity to teach children about half, quarter and whole. Count the number of orange slices given to each child out loud and encourage children to count as well.

Sensory Play

Add rice to the sensory table and tools such as measuring cups, shovels, spoons, and plates. To add color to the sensory table, take batches of rice, divide it into four sections, and pour it into bowls. Add different food coloring to each section. Mix well. Let it dry over paper towel before adding it to the table.

 **Game Play**

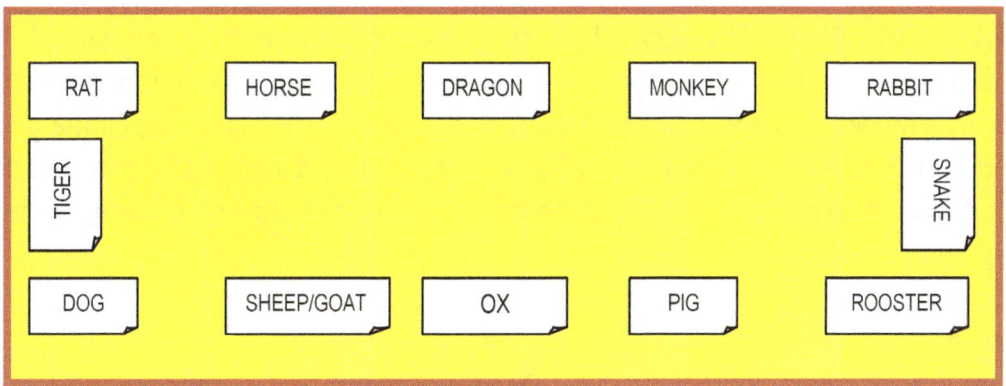

Animal Guessing Game: Make an animal board using all the animals from the Chinese New Year Zodiac. Cut strips of paper, fold them in half, and glue inside each strip a picture of an animal. On the front flap, write simple descriptive clues such as: *Sniffs, barks, and has to dig out bones to eat. Guess who it is?* Read out loud and let the child guess the animal.

Writing Center

Provide children with diamond-shaped paper, crayons, markers, yarn, stickers and other craft materials. Ask children to decorate their paper to make a kite. Punch a hole on one side of the kite and string a long thread of yarn. Tie the yarn to the paper. Let children hold the kite by the yarn and swing it in the air.

Dramatic Play

Provide children with child-sized brooms, dust pans, pretend vacuum cleaners, dusters and rag cloths to sweep the area. Read again one of the children's books about Chinese New Year and point out all the preparations done before the celebration such us cleaning the house to sweep away bad luck.

Day #2

Art Activity

Fireworks: Make fireworks by using dark blue construction paper, glitter, paints of different colors and a sponge paint wand (or use a kitchen duster). Ask children to dip the wand in the paint and sweep it all over the paper. Sprinkle glitter on the paint and slide the excess glitter off the picture into a paper plate to use for the next child. A variation of this activity is to use a straw instead of the wand to blow the paint across the paper.

Circle Time

Establish a Circle Time routine. Read <u>Lanterns and Firecrackers</u> by Johnny Zucker. After reading the book, ask children to describe how they made fireworks and to compare their projects to fireworks seen during the holidays. Write their responses on chart paper.

Music Time

Place children in a circle to sing and act out the following song:

THIS IS THE WAY…

Sung to: This is the Way…

This is the way we dance and turn,
Dance and turn,
Dance and turn
This is the way we dance in turn
Every Chinese Year…

Jacqueline Lopez

Substitute *dance and turn* for *clap and jump; laugh and play*, etc.

Movement

Play a CD with Chinese traditional music. Let children move to the beat and dance around the classroom. To add more fun to the dance, provide children with ribbon, streamers or fans and encourage them to use them as they dance.

Math Activity

Domino cards: Make domino cards by printing numbers from one to five (*as children get older you can add numbers six to ten*). Create a second set of cards with the corresponding domino dots. Feel free to make multiple sets of number and dot cards. To make it easier for children to match the cards, color-code the background of each card and use a different color for each number (i.e. for one dot use orange, for two dots use blue…). Laminate. Shuffle and place the cards in a pile face down on the table. Let one child pick a card, turn it face up, and place it on the table. Then ask another child to pick another card from the pile and observe if the card matches the one on the table. Let children continue taking turns until a child picks the correct card. Continue until all children have a turn and all cards are played.

Building with blocks

Let children sort all the Unifix blocks by color and leave out only the red ones. Let children build, make patterns or simply make towers with these blocks.

Day #3

Art Activity

Finger-painting with red: Provide children with smocks, red finger-paint and paper. Place a spoonful of red paint on the table and let the children spread the paint. When ready, place the paper on top of the paint to make a print. For better results, let children use their fingers to draw pictures with the paint, write their names or simply draw lines before adding the paper to make a print.

Circle Time

Establish a Circle Time routine. Read Big Red Barn by Margaret Wise_Brown. After reading the book, ask children to name objects that are red. If a child can't think of anything, ask him/her to look around the classroom and point to something that is red. Write their responses on chart paper.

Writing Center

Provide different shades of red paper, red envelopes, markers and crayons, scissors, glue, old magazines and scraps of paper. Encourage children to draw, cut or tear out pictures and paste it on the paper. When dried, let children fold the paper and slide it into the red envelope and give it to a friend as a token of friendship.

Science Activity

Catching lucky coins: This activity will help children learn about the principles of magnetism. Provide children with a magnetic wand and coins. Wave the wand over the coins to see if they are magnetic. This activity needs to be done with close adult supervision since children can put the coins in their mouths. As a variation, provide children with magnetic marbles, chips, and paper clips. Also provide children with non-magnetic items to observe and compare how a magnetic field works. Adult supervision is required throughout the activity.

Sensory Play

Provide children with play-dough and cutting tools. Encourage children to make wonton chips by rolling the dough and cutting it into small strips to resemble Chinese chips. Use a play-dough "pasta" maker (dough presses) to make "spaghetti."

Finger Play

Recite the following rhyme with the children:

HERE IS THE DRAGON

Here is the castle but where is the dragon?
(Hold up fist)
Flying away where nobody can see.
(Move other hand over fist)
Watch and you will see him jumping out of nowhere
(Bend head close to clasped hands)
One, two, three, four, five,
(Hold fingers up one at a time)
Thump...it ran away!
(Wave fingers)

Jacqueline Lopez

Water Play

Fill up the sensory table with water. Add red food coloring and swirl until dissolved. Collect red items and ask children to drop them in the water. A variation of this activity is to make "red" ice cubes by pouring previously colored red water into ice trays. Place the ice trays in the freezer overnight. Add the ice cubes to the water table and watch them melt and turn the water in the water table red.

Day #4

Art Activity

Chinese Fans: Provide children with paper plates, tissue paper cut in small triangles, craft sticks and glue. Cut the paper plates in half and let children glue the tissue paper to the paper plate "fan." Attach a craft stick for easy handling.

Circle Time

Establish a Circle Time routine. Read <u>One Red Rooster</u> by Kathleen Sullivan. After reading the book, ask children to name all animals portrayed in the story and to make the sounds associated with each animal. Write their responses on chart paper.

Game Play

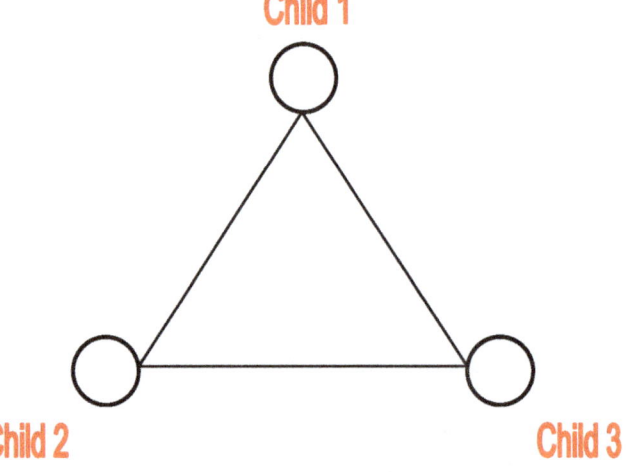

Triangle Game: This activity can be performed indoors or outdoors. Ask three children to sit in such a way as to form a triangle (see diagram). Give a child a ball and encourage him to throw the ball to the second child; the second child will then throw the ball to the third child. To make this activity a learning experience, sit three children on a large piece of butcher paper. Dip a small ball in paint. Ask children to roll the ball to each other until the triangle shape is formed on the paper.

Field Trip

Visit a pet store. Observe the goldfish. In Chinese culture, goldfish symbolize good fortune. If possible, buy a goldfish to keep as a pet in the class. Allow children to feed the goldfish once a day.

Snack Idea

Red Snack: Serve red foods such as strawberries, tomatoes, or cranberry juice. Also prepare red Jell-O by following the recipe on the box. Refrigerate. Use a triangle-shaped cookie cutter to cut small triangles out of Jell-O. To extend this activity, let children make their own triangle placemats by cutting sheets of construction paper into triangles and decorating them as desired. Laminate the placemats.

Writing Center

Triangle Book: Cut out paper of different colors into triangles. Provide children with markers, crayons, scraps of paper, glue, scissors and other materials. Loop all the papers together to make a class triangle book.

Math Activity

Red sorting: Provide children with a large container, craft sticks, and colorful Unifix blocks. Ask children to sort the blocks by using two craft sticks as "chopsticks" to grab and place the blocks in the container.

Day #5

Art Activity

Triangle collages: Provide children with sheets of construction paper and glue. Cut small triangles out of tissue paper, crepe paper, gift wrap and felt. Place pom-poms in a bowl. Have children spread glue on the paper and then let them place the triangles on top of the paper. Additionally, encourage children to take the pom-poms and form a triangle shape. A variation of this activity is to pre-cut sandpaper and card stock into triangle shapes. Glue these shapes to a piece of cardboard. Lay wax paper or any other thin paper over the cardboard. Ask children to turn the crayon sideways and rub over the triangle shapes to make colorful designs.

Circle Time

Establish a Circle Time routine. Read The Greedy Triangle by Marilyn Burns. After reading the book, ask children to name the places or items where triangles can be found in the story. Write their responses in a chart.

Finger Play

Photocopy pages of the story The Greedy Triangle. Cut out the pictures and laminate them. Attach a Velcro piece (or tape) to the back. Put on a felt glove (or a disposable glove). Recreate the events in the story by placing the pictures on each finger. This is a good memory exercise for young children. Leave the pieces on a felt board or in a box for children to use.

Game Play

Buddy Triangles: Use pieces of masking tape to outline triangle shapes in the playground. Let children take turns jumping, hopping, and walking from one triangle to another. Have children lay on the triangular outlines and make the triangle shape with their own bodies. Ask children how many children are needed to make one triangle.

Science Activity

Planting a Bamboo: Use a pot with adequate room for the bamboo to grow. Add potting-soil and moisten the soil. Make a hole in the middle of the soil and place the bamboo. Cover and add more soil if needed. Keep the plant near a window. Avoid direct sunlight as it will scorch the leaves. Water the plant once a week.

Writing Center

Provide children with triangle cutouts, craft sticks, stickers, markers, glue and crayons. Ask children to decorate the triangles and glue them to the craft sticks to create a prop for the Movement Activity below.

Movement

Use Sing & Read Shape Collection Shape CD to play "Trixie Triangle." Ask children to sing and act out this lively song. Encourage children to lift up the previously made triangle cutouts and to shake them as they dance.

Math Activity

Lacing Cards: Make triangle-shaped lacing cards. Cut small, medium and large triangles out of sheets of color construction paper. Punch holes around the shapes. Help children string around the triangle shapes. Point out the different sizes and colors.

January

Winter

Parent Letter
JANUARY NEWS

Dear Parents,

A New Year has come which means the beginning of new activities as well. The winter weather is perfect for playing in the snow and making a snowman. This month, we will focus our unit on all winter activities (indoors and outdoors), winter clothing, winter animals and we will finish our unit on hibernation.

As always, we will divide this theme into four simple segments, which are the following:

- Winter
- Winter animals, color blue
- Winter clothes, winter sports
- Hibernation, rectangle shape

Some of the learning activities planned for this month include:

- Creating a winter collage
- Experiencing snow and ice in the sensory table
- Adding winter clothing to the dramatic play area
- Adding snowflake stickers on wooden boards for sorting
- Making a squirrel home
- Creating ice-skating prints
- Reciting the poem, "The Three Little Kittens"
- Making number cards

We are looking forward to working on this theme and learning about all winter activities, especially those activities that help children explore the world around them such as experiencing snow and ice in the sensory table. Our intention is to create awareness of all the changes that take place during winter season.

PLANNING WEB
Week #1

Learning Center: SOCIAL • Divide children into two groups. Ask children to list things they do in winter time. Share their responses with the class	**Learning Center: MATH** • <u>Count snowflakes</u>: Write numbers on snowflakes	**Learning Center: LANGUAGE/BOOKS** • <u>There was Some Lady who Swallowed Some Snow</u> by Lucille Collandro • <u>Emmett's Snowball</u> by Ned Miller	**Group Time** <u>Small Group</u>: • Play with winter puzzles <u>Large Group</u>: • Play "Freeze and Unfreeze"
Learning Center: DRAMATIC PLAY • Add winter clothes to the dramatic play area	**Developmental Goal:** • Develop an understanding of the winter season and related activities • Help children acquire confidence and self-control in solving problems and challenges on their own **Story/Theme:** • <u>The Mitten</u> by Jan Brett **Diversity:** • Display winter pictures around the world		**Routines/Transitions** <u>Gathering Game</u>: • Children will line up by stepping on their initials which are taped to the floor
Learning Center: ART/MUSIC/MOVEMENT • Cotton ball snow people • Coffee filter snowflakes • "Five Little Snowflakes" rhyme • Pass the Ice Cube Game	**INDOORS OUTDOORS** <u>Indoors</u>: • Color with winter colors <u>Outdoors</u>: • Play the "Pass the Ice" game	**Health/Nutrition/Cooking** • Remind parents to dress children appropriately for the cold weather	**Learning Center: SCIENCE/SENSORY** • Catch snowflakes (Science) • Add snow cubes to the water table

CLASS GOAL

Week #1

LEARN ABOUT SNOW
AND
WINTER

Day #1

Art Activity

Cotton ball snow-people: Set up the art table with black sheets of construction paper, glue, white paint, white dot-paints, cotton balls and paper plates. Pour the paint on the plates. Ask children to dip the cotton balls in the paint and press them on the paper. Ask children to overlap the balls to create tall and short snowmen. Use the white dot-paint to add snowflakes around the paper. Older children can add face features to the snowmen.

Circle Time

Start Circle Time by gathering all children in a circle. Read <u>There was Some Lady who Swallowed Some Snow</u> by Lucille Collandro. Ask children if they think a person could swallow snow, a pipe, coal, a hat and a stick as in the story. Write down their responses on chart paper.

Water Play

Look for plastic small containers with lids. Insert a toy in the container. Fill up with water and freeze overnight. Unmold and place the frozen toy in the water table. Provide children with plastic spoons to swirl the ice cubes. Observe how the ice melts and frees the toy. To accelerate the melting process, spray salt over the frozen toys.

Finger Play

Make a prop to retell the story above. Make a simple outline of a lady out of cardboard. Copy the face of an old lady and glue it on the cardboard. Use wall paper or colorful sheets of construction paper to design clothes. Attach a Ziploc bag in her tummy. Add legs and arms. Copy and laminate images of all items swallowed. Allow children to retell the story using these props.

Game Play

Ice Cube Hockey: This activity can be played outdoors over a table. Select two players. Use tape to make a red line at one end of the table and a blue line at the other end. Provide each player with a spoon. Set an ice cube in the middle of the table. Players will battle to get the ice cube past the goalie line using the spoons. They cannot use their hands to help move the cube. The game will continue until all players have a turn. If desired, add one or two drops of food coloring to the ice tray and use different colors for each player.

Puzzle

Snowman puzzle: Copy pictures of a snowman or a class picture of children playing in the snow on letter-sized paper. Glue the paper on a colorful sheet of construction paper. Decide how many puzzle pieces you would like to make. Cut out and laminate each piece. Glue the pieces onto cardboard for extended play and cut off the extra cardboard.

Snack Idea

Iced cup: Gather blue Kool-Aid, ginger ale soda, vanilla ice cream, drinking cup, whipped cream, chopped ice in a blender (put ice cubes in the blender until they are chopped) and straw. In a bowl, mix half a cup of ginger ale, half a cup of Kool-Aid, and the ice. Mix well. Adjust the portions according to the number of children. Serve this mixture in individual cups. Decorate by adding a scoop of vanilla ice cream and whipped cream. Add a cherry on top.

Day #2

Art Activity

Winter Scene: Provide children with blue or black construction paper. Look for small twigs or use pipe cleaners instead. When using twigs, make sure they have no sharp ends. Hold the twigs upright and thread cotton balls through the twigs. Continue until the twig is covered with cotton balls. Glue the twig to the paper. Add snowflake stickers or small dots of white paint to simulate falling snow in the scene. A variation of this activity is to place the twig in a small terracotta pot. Add potting soil to the pot. Decorate the pot with snowflake stickers.

Circle Time

Start Circle Time by gathering all children in a circle. To introduce the story, ask the children to name some of their favorite activities in the snow. Read Frozen Noses by Jan Carr. After reading the story, ask children to list some of the activities the characters tried in the story. Write down their responses on chart paper.

Writing Center

Paper Snowman: Cut multiple small, medium and large circles. Provide children with blue construction paper, markers, crayons and glue. Ask children to glue the circles to the paper, keeping the largest one on the bottom, medium in the middle and smallest on top. Children can draw faces, hats, arms, bottoms, etc. to complete the snowman.

Snack Idea

Edible igloo: Provide children with a round cookie, marshmallow chunks and marshmallow fluff. Spread marshmallow fluff all over the cookie and place the chunks next to one another to form an igloo. A variation of this activity is to substitute the cookie for a cupcake.

Puzzle

Make an outline of a child. Laminate. Draw or cut out winter clothes (sweatshirts, sweatpants, scarves, mittens, gloves, hats, etc.) from construction paper. Laminate. Encourage children to dress and undress their "doll."

Finger Play

Make props to recite this rhyme. Make a copy of snowmen pictures and laminate them. Attach a craft stick to the back of the picture. Sit children in a circle to recite the following rhyme:

FIVE LITTLE SNOWMEN

Five little snowmen skating in a row,
One went to the store and then there were only four.

Four little snowmen skating in a row,
One bumped into a tree and then there were only three.

Three little snowmen skating in a row,
One got the flu and then there were only two.

Two little snowmen skating in a row,
One stayed under the sun and then there was only one

One little snowman skating in a row,
He melted and then there were none.

Jacqueline Lopez

Day #3

Art Activity

Coffee Filter Snowflakes: Provide children with coffee filters, bright color markers, glue, water spray bottle, scissors, paint brush and glitter. Have the children draw designs on the coffee filter by using the markers. Spray water on the filter to allow the colors to run. Let the filter dry. Spread a thin layer of glue and sprinkle glitter. Let it dry again. Help children fold and cut the coffee filter into a snowflake shape.

Circle Time

Establish a Circle Time routine. Read <u>The Gingerbread Man</u> by Catherine McCafferty. After reading the story, ask children to list all the characters in the story that were following the gingerbread man. Write down their responses on chart paper.

Science Activity

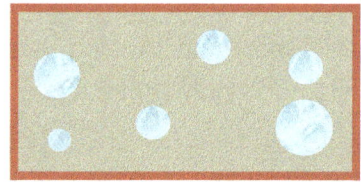

Freeze Bubbles: Buy Gymboree brand bubbles (at Party City or any other party supply store). Using a bubble wand, blow bubbles over a piece of cardboard. Notice how these bubbles do not pop and last longer. Freeze the bubbles for a longer lasting effect. Observe how bubbles look like crystal glass. A variation of this activity is to blow regular bubbles on a cold winter day. Catch the bubbles on a piece of cardboard and watch them freeze. Watch how the bubbles turn into ice. Use different wand sizes to blow bubbles.

Dramatic Play
Add a tent to the dramatic play area and convert it into an igloo by taping bubble wrapping paper all around the tent. Add a basket with winter clothes: hats, mittens, scarves, etc. and add dolls for children to dress up.

Game Play
Pass the Ice: Sit children in a circle. Similar to "Hot Potato," turn the music on and ask children to pass an ice cube around as fast as they can. When the music stops, ask the children to talk about how the ice feels.

Snack Idea
Make a gingerbread house. Provide children with graham crackers, cornflakes, dried fruit, icing and powdered sugar. Children will use the icing to "glue" graham crackers together to make a roof and walls. Add more icing to the roof to stick the cornflakes. Use the dried fruit to decorate the walls. When finished, sprinkle powdered sugar all over to represent snow.

Sensory Play
Gingerbread people: Add gingerbread cookie cutters of different sizes to the sensory table. Provide children with a batch of play-dough. Let children mold the play-dough and use the cookie cutters to make gingerbread men.

Writing Center
Cut gingerbread man shapes out of sandpaper. Provide children with paper, crayons, and markers. Tape the sandpaper cutout to the table. Place a piece of paper on top of the cutout and let children rub a brown crayon until the shape appears. Let children use markers or crayons of different colors to add features like eyes, nose, mouth, etc. For older children, provide scissors so they can cut out the gingerbread man.

Day #4

Art Activity

Ice Cube Painting: Provide children with powdered tempera paint, popsicle sticks, foam bowls or any small containers, spoons and an ice cube tray. Fill up the tray with water. Use a popsicle stick as a handle and place one in each compartment of the tray. Freeze. Add one or two spoons of dry tempera paint to the foam bowls. Lay a sheet of paper on the table, and let children scoop little amounts of the tempera paint and spread it all over the paper. Unmold the ice cubes and allow children to slide the ice around the paint to make colorful designs. Dry and display.

Circle Time

Establish a Circle Time routine. Read <u>Emmett's Snowball</u> by Ned Miller. After reading the story, ask children if they have ever made snowballs as big as Emmett's or to describe their favorite part of the story. Write their responses on chart paper.

Building with blocks

Display pictures of a gingerbread house, igloos, icebergs, Lego people, winter animals, etc. Let children use their imaginations to recreate these pictures using blocks.

Math Activity

Count Snowflakes: Make numbered snowflake cards out of colorful sheets of construction paper. Laminate.

 **Music Time**

Let children stand up in a circle to sing the following song. Encourage children to act out the movements.

THIS IS THE WAY
Sung to the tune of: This is the Way

This is the way we put on our coats,
Put on our coats, put on our coats,
This is the way we put on our coats,
Every winter morning.

This is the way we wear our scarves,
Wear our scarves, wear our scarves.
This is the way we wear our scarves,
Snug on our neck.

This is the way we slide on our boots,
Slide on our boots, slide on our boots,
This is the way we slide on our boots,
To keep our feet warm.

Jacqueline Lopez

Snack Idea

<u>Snow drink</u>: Put ice in a blender, crush it and place it in small cups. Pour fruit juice over the ice and serve for snack. Provide children with straws to stir and sip the juice.

Day #5

Art Activity

Mitten Wreath: Trace the children's hands on a sheet of color construction paper. Use different colors for each child. Cut a mitten shape out of their traced hands. Provide children with snow stickers and let them decorate their mittens as they wish. Stretch a hanger into a circle shape and place the mittens on the hanger to create a mitten wreath.

Circle Time

Establish a Circle Time routine. Read <u>The Mitten</u> by Jan Brett. After reading the story, ask children to recall the number of animals that went into the mitten. How would it feel to be in the mitten with all the animals? Write their responses on chart paper.

Math Activity

Mix and Match Math Activity: Take pictures of the children's mittens (right and left separately) and paste them on a sheet of construction paper. Use different color construction paper for each child. Laminate. Spread all the pictures on the table. Let children match all pictures according to color, design, etc.

Writing Center

Cut mitten, boot, coat, and hat shapes (to name a few shapes) out of a sturdy piece of construction paper or cardboard. Laminate or cover with contact paper (if you use construction paper). Punch holes around the shapes. Provide children with string and let children thread the string around these shapes.

Finger Play

Find an adult-sized wool mitten. Copy pictures of all the animals displayed in the story <u>The Mitten</u>. Laminate. Use these props to help children retell the story.

Science Activity

Melting Ice: Set up the table with two dry bowls, two trays of ice cubes, and salt. Let children empty one tray in bowl one. Sprinkle salt over the ice cubes. Observe and record how long it takes for all the ice cubes to melt. Write the melting time on a chart. Then, add ice cubes to bowl two. Let the bowl sit at room temperature and compare the melting times. Write down the observations.

Water Play

Make Snow: Find Instant-Snow in an Arts & Craft Store. Follow the container instructions to mix the powder with water to create fluffy snow. This is a great resource especially when children don't have the opportunity to play, see or touch real snow. Provide children with shovels, measuring containers of different sizes and small plastic winter animals such as polar bears, frogs, chipmunks, frogs, etc., for extended play.

PLANNING WEB
Week #2

Learning Center: SOCIAL - Pair up children in the group. Tape a large piece of irregularly-shaped blue paper to the carpet. Provide children with blocks, and plastic animal figures to build homes for the arctic animals. Ask children to describe their actions	**Learning Center: MATH** - <u>Whale Bar Graph:</u> Measure child's height. - Sorting blue items	**Learning Center: LANGUAGE/BOOKS** - <u>Little Polar Bear Finds a Friend</u> by Hans de Beer - <u>One Winter's Day</u> by M. Christina Butler	**Group Time** <u>Small Group:</u> - Display an assortment of blue crayons and paper for children to draw and color <u>Large Group:</u> - Pretend skating game activity
Learning Center: DRAMATIC PLAY - Transform the dramatic play area into a winter animal habitat	**Developmental Goal:** - Provide indoor space for children to play and interact with one another. Encourage children to read books and share stories in quiet areas such as inside a tent in a reading corner **Story/Theme:** - <u>Ollie's Ski Trip</u> by Elsa Beskow. **Diversity:** - Display pictures of winter scenes around the world		**Routines/Transitions** - Children will put their coats on without assistance by placing the coat on the floor, putting their arms in the coat and flipping the coat over their heads
Learning Center: ART/MUSIC/MOVEMENT - Winter animal stencils - Piñata Igloo - "Bear Went Over the Mountain" song	**INDOORS OUTDOORS** <u>Indoors</u>: - Make Frost <u>Outdoors</u>: - Go for a blue color hunt around the school	**Health/Nutrition/Cooking** - Make blue sandwiches	**Learning Center: SCIENCE/SENSORY** - Add blue food coloring and blue toys to the water table. - Make play-dough cookies

CLASS GOAL

Week #2

LEARN ABOUT WINTER ANIMALS
AND
THE COLOR BLUE

Day #1

Art Activity
Winter Animals Stencil:

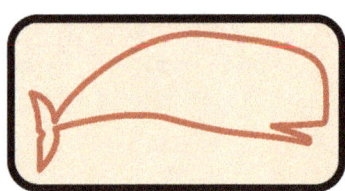 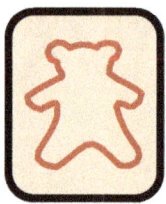

Provide children with sea lion, whale, penguin, polar bear and other winter animal stencils or make original stencils by drawing the shape of an animal on different textures (bubble wrap, corrugated paper, etc.). Cut the shape out and provide children with crayons or paint to rub or paint over the shapes.

Circle Time
Start Circle Time by gathering all children in a circle. Read <u>Little Polar Bear Finds a Friend</u> by Hans de Beer. Ask children about their favorite part of the story. Write down their responses on chart paper.

Game Play
Make ice skates. Collect cardboard egg trays. Tape an egg tray under each shoe. Make sure the egg tray is only slightly bigger than the child's shoe by cutting off any excess. To further secure the egg tray to the shoe, poke two holes on the left and right edges of the tray. Make a safety band by threading a pipe cleaner over the shoes. Then, ask children to move and glide their bodies.

Dramatic Play

Transform the dramatic play area into a winter animal habitat. Add photos of polar bears, whales, hares, etc., books, and plastic toys for extended play.

Building with blocks

Tape a large piece of irregularly-shaped blue paper to the carpet. Encourage children to work on top of the paper. Provide children with blocks and plastic animal figures to build homes for the arctic animals.

Music Time

Invite children to sit or stand in a circle and sing the following song.

THE BEAR WENT OVER THE MOUNTAIN
(Song)

The bear went over the mountain,
The bear went over the mountain,
The bear went over the mountain,
   To see what he could see

To see what he could see,
To see what he could see

The other side of the mountain,
The other side of the mountain,
The other side of the mountain,
   Was all that he could see

Was all that he could see,
Was all that he could see,
The other side of the mountain,
   Was all that he could see!

Traditional

Day #2

 **Art Activity**

Creating a Piñata Igloo: Wear a smock. Cover the art table with newspaper. Set up the area with flour and water or glue, newspaper, white construction paper and a large balloon. Help children tear old newspapers into strips. Tear enough pieces to make at least three layers to cover the piñata. Use regular glue or make a glue paste by mixing in a bowl two cups of flour and one cup of water. Add more flour if the paste is too watery or more water if the paste is too hard. Blow and tie a balloon. Dip the strips of newspaper into the paste, leaving out the excess and press them on the balloon. Cover the balloon with at least 3 layers, allowing each layer to dry a lit bit before applying the next. Cut rectangular shapes out of white construction paper and glue them to the piñata. You can also paint on the rectangles using white acrylic or fabric paint. Let the piñata dry overnight and then pop the balloon. Cut an opening in front. If desired, substitute the balloon for a ball to make the piñata shown in the picture.

Circle Time

Establish a Circle Time routine. Read One Winter's Day by M. Christina Butler. After reading the story, ask the children what would happen if the wind blew their house down as in the story. Can they list all the animals the hedgehog (main character) met and helped along the way? Write their responses on chart paper.

Water Play

Fill up the water table. Add and swirl blue food coloring. Ask children to look for plastic items that are blue and drop them in the table.

Math Activity

Whale Bar Graph: Make copies of whale pictures and glue them to an index card. Make at least ten cards. Let children stand against the wall to measure their height. Stack and tape the whale cards to record the children's height. Use different winter animals (sea lion, polar bear, hare, walrus, and penguin) to record the height of every child. If the number of children is greater than the number of animals available, use pictures of the animals' habitats.

Cooking Idea

Play-dough Cookies: Make different animal shapes out of play-dough using a cookie cutter. Make a hole at the top of each shape. Grease a baking sheet and spread out the shapes. Pre-heat the oven at 300°F for ten minutes. Bake the cookies for ten to fifteen minutes or until dry. The cooking process should not exceed twenty minutes or the cookies will crack. Add white tempera paint to three different small bowls. Add one spoon of blue paint to the first bowl, two spoons of blue paint to the second bowl and finally, three spoons of blue paint to the third bowl. Mix well. Paint the cookies using any of the different shades of blue. Let them dry. Thread yarn through the holes to make a cookie garland. Display the garland on a window.

Day #3

Art Activity

Swirling Paint: Because this can be a messy project, cover the table with newspaper or a plastic tablecloth. Fill a large aluminum baking pan with water. Add ¼ cup of baby oil and ¼ cup of blue tempera paint to the pan. Stir gently with a craft stick. Lay a piece of white construction paper on the water. Wait a couple of seconds before removing the paper. Lay the paper flat to dry over sheets of newspaper. Turn constantly from side to side until it dries.

Circle Time

Start Circle Time by gathering all children in a circle. Read <u>Ollie's Ski Trip</u> by Elsa Beskow. Ask children to list all of the winter characters Ollie ran into in the woods. Write down their responses on chart paper.

Science Activity

Making Frost: Set up the sensory table with the following materials: sheet of paper, empty coffee can, crushed ice, and salt. Fill the can halfway with crushed ice. Lay the paper on the table. Spray water until the paper is wet. Place the can on top of the paper. Fill up the remainder of the can with salt. Mix the ice and salt well. Record the amount of time it takes for frost to appear outside the can.

Sensory Play

Fill the sensory table with blue rice. To dye the rice, use a large Ziploc bag and add blue coloring. Shake well. Let the rice air dry overnight.

Show and Tell
Ask children to wear something blue or to bring to school an item that is blue for Show and Tell. Encourage children to stand up and describe the item in their own words.

Math Activity
Sorting blue items: Place colorful items on a table such as blocks, toys, pompoms, etc. Let children look for and separate all items that are blue. Then encourage children to count how many items they found.

Writing Center
Staple several white pages to make a book. Use blue paper as a cover. Write "My Blue Book" and the child's name on the front cover. Help children look through magazines or catalogs and tear or cut out blue pictures. Then have the children glue the pictures on the sheets of paper. If the children have trouble finding pictures, provide blue construction paper of different shades for them to tear and paste. Additionally, supply children with crayons or markers to decorate their books.

Field Trip
Take the children for a walk around the school or the neighborhood. Look for blue signs, blue cars, people wearing blue, etc.

Sand Play
Coloring Sand: Provide each child with a container that has a lid. Help them fill the container with a few drops of food coloring and some water. Pour sand in the container. Place the lid on the container. Shake hard. Let the sand sit for a while, moving it occasionally to ensure that the sand dyes evenly. Empty the containers into the sand table. Provide children with empty small jars or bottles, cookie cutters, shovels, spoons, measuring cups, etc. so they can play and mold different figures with the sand.

Day #4

Art Activity

Dripping Paint: Provide children with small paper cups, blue tempera paint, a pitcher of water, an empty pitcher and paper. Pour paint into the empty pitcher. Add water to the paint pitcher until the paint is thin. Poke small holes in the paper cups. Cover the table with a large sheet of butcher paper. Let children hold the cups over the paper and pour the water and paint mixture into the cups. Rotate the cups gently so the paint drips on the paper.

Circle Time

Start Circle Time by gathering all children in a circle. Read Color Zoo by Lois Ehlert. Ask children to recall all the animals and colors presented in the book. Write down their responses on chart paper.

Snack Idea

Blue Sandwiches: Place one spoon of cream cheese into a paper cup. Add one drop of blue food coloring. Mix well. Smear bread with cream cheese. Serve the sandwiches with blueberries on the side.

Finger Play

Recite the following rhyme about blue color.

BLUE

Peek-a boo, who is wearing blue.
_____ is wearing red, white and blue.
Says who?
The boy who lost a shoe
Who sneezes ah-choo...!

Jacqueline Lopez

Movement

Play a CD. Dance to the music. When the music stops, have the children find a friend or look for a toy that has something blue. Turn the music back on and dance again, stopping when the music stops to hunt for blue. For extra fun, provide children with blue streamers for them to twirl and dance.

Penguin Magnetic Puzzle

Cut several shapes out of construction paper: a large oval for the body; one medium sized circle for the stomach, two small ovals for feet, two triangle shapes for the arms, one orange triangle for the beak and two circles for the eyes. Make two sets of these pieces. Glue one set together to be used as a puzzle board. Place the loose pieces of the second set on the board to complete the puzzle. If you wish, glue pieces of magnetic strips to the backs of all the loose pieces and display the puzzle on a magnetic board.

Day #5

Art Activity:

Making a Penguin: This is a good activity to review shapes with children. Provide each child with a large oval shape made out of black construction paper and a medium-sized oval shape made out of a white construction paper. Encourage children to tear black pieces of construction paper and black tissue paper, and place them (and other objects such as black pom-poms) on the black oval paper. Glue white collage material to the white circle paper. Provide the children with googly eyes, orange construction paper ovals for legs, and small white triangles pieces for arms. Observe if children can glue these accordingly. To make the activity easier, display pictures of penguins for children to observe and copy.

Circle Time

Start Circle Time by gathering all children in a circle. Read <u>I Am Not Scared</u> by Jonathan Allen. Ask children if they have ever felt afraid when their parents are not around. Do they have a trusty toy like Owly? Can they name all the animals he met along the way? Write their responses on chart paper.

Dramatic Play

Ask children to bring an extra set of blue clothes to school such as gloves, scarves, shirts, and pants to wear and dress-up in blue.

Water Play

Add blue food coloring to the water table. Add winter water animals such as whales, baby belugas, sea lions, and penguins.

Snack Idea

Blue Kool-Aid Drink: Add 1/2 cup of water to a pitcher. Add blue Kool-Aid powdered mix and sugar. Mix well. Pour the mixture in small cups. Add ice chunks and blueberries for extra flavor.

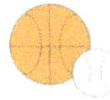 ## Art Activity 2

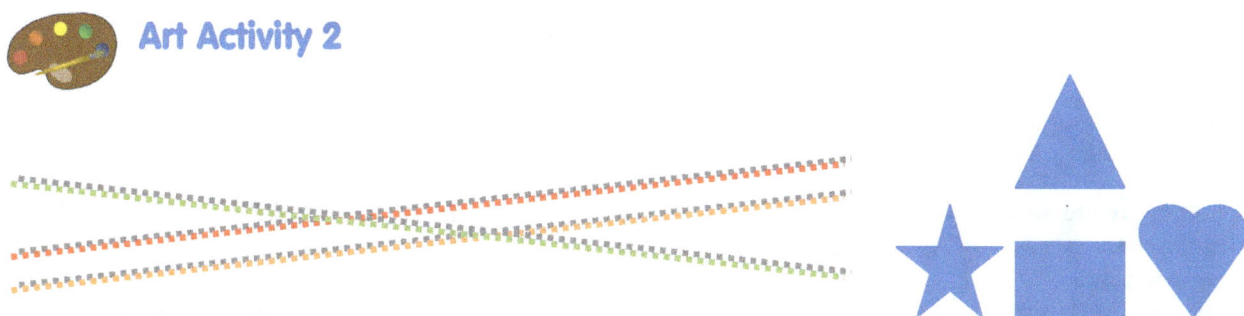

Provide children with blue construction paper, scissors and pipe cleaners. Ask children to tear or cut the paper into different small shapes. Give each child a pipe cleaner and help children insert the pipe cleaner through each shape to make a blue paper necklace. For extra fun, substitute the paper for blue cereal loops to make an edible necklace.

Game Play

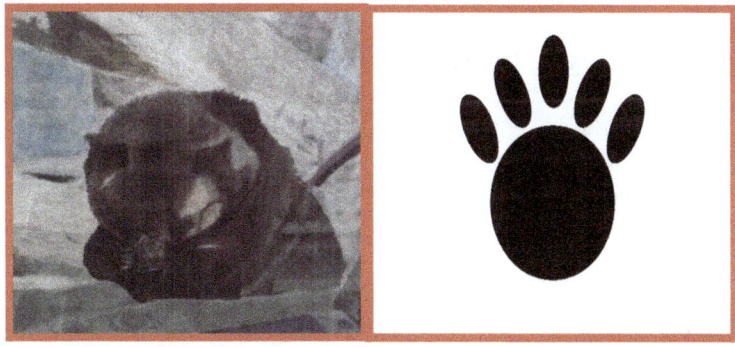

Step on the Footprints: Print winter animal footprints on one half of an index card and the picture of the animal on the other half of the card. Make sure to include as many winter animals as possible – owl, penguin, whale, polar bear, hare, etc. Laminate the cards. Tape them to the floor or the carpet so they are not slippery. Have the children hop like a hare, flap their wings like an eagle, or growl like a polar bear when they move from one footprint to the next.

PLANNING WEB
Week #3

Learning Center: SOCIAL - Ask children to list all of the clothing they wear to play outdoors. Give each child the opportunity to describe what he/she wears	**Learning Center: MATH** - Use mitten cutouts to measure items.	**Learning Center: LANGUAGE/BOOKS** - <u>The Three Little Kittens</u> by Laura Ferraro - <u>The Hat</u> by Jan Brett	**Group Time** **Small Group:** - Make a squirrel puzzle **Large Group:** - Act out "The Three Little Kittens" poem
Learning Center: DRAMATIC PLAY - Add a tent to the dramatic area to create a "cave reading corner." Add books about winter and winter animals and outdoor winter clothing	**Developmental Goal:** - Include outdoor play time in morning and afternoon play - Encourage children to exchange ideas in casual conversations by showing or displaying pictures of animals and their winter homes **Story/Theme:** - <u>Froggy Gets Dressed</u> by Jonathan London **Diversity:** - Display pictures of winter locomotion: sled, toboggan, skis, snowmobile, etc.		**Routines/Transitions** - Talk to the children about the reasons we wear coats - Practice with children how to put on and take off their coats
Learning Center: ART/MUSIC/MOVEMENT - Handprint Mittens - Recite "The Three Little Kittens" - Winter animals collage	**INDOORS OUTDOORS** **Indoors:** - Make a squirrel den **Outdoors:** - Go for a squirrel hunt	**Health/Nutrition/Cooking** - Bake mitten-shaped cookies	**Learning Center: SCIENCE/SENSORY** - Add crushed ice to the water table - Create a squirrel habitat

CLASS GOAL

Week #3

LEARN ABOUT WINTER CLOTHING, OTHER WINTER ANIMALS AND WINTER SPORTS

Day #1

Art Activity

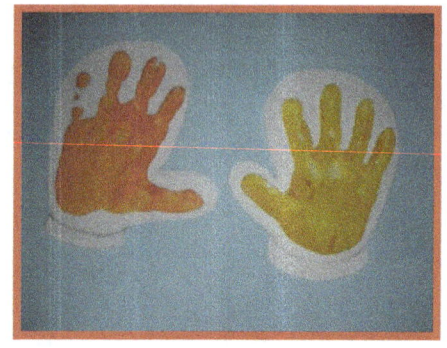

Handprint Mittens: Provide children with color construction paper, markers, paints of different colors and paintbrushes. Children will create their own mittens by tracing their hands on a sheet of paper. The children should trace their thumbs, and then their remaining four fingers collectively (so that the resulting shape will resemble a mitten). Cut the mittens out and help children decorate their mittens. They can tear pieces of color construction paper and glue them to the mittens. Poke a hole in the mittens' cuffs to string yarn and tie the mittens together. A variation of this activity is to paint the children's hands to create a handprint on white paper. Cut out the white paper to create mittens.

Circle Time

Start Circle Time by gathering all children in a circle. Read <u>Three Little Kittens</u> by Laura Ferraro. Ask children about the number of times the kittens got into trouble. Do they finally make amends and get to eat the pie? Write down their responses on chart paper.

Cooking Idea

Mitten cookies: Make cookie-dough by following a box recipe. Flatten the dough. Using a mitten cookie cutter, roll out the dough and make mitten cookies. Bake and let cool. Decorate the cookies with frosting and sprinkles.

Math Activity

Use pre-cut mitten shapes to measure the length of different items in the class.

Finger Play

Let children recite and act out the following rhyme. Provide children with a large string of yarn. Allow them to crawl and purr like a cat while they move the string around them.

THE THREE LITTLE KITTENS

Three little kittens
Soft, warm and playful
Rolled a ball of yarn
Around and around
Until they were
Wrapped around
Help, said the kittens
Just move around, said the mom
And the three little kittens
Spun around and around
Until they were
Finally unbound!

Jacqueline Lopez

Game Play

Mitten in a line: Trace and cut mittens out of felt. Cut small shapes out of colorful felt and let children glue these pieces to their mitten to decorate as they wish. Place two removable adhesive hooks on an empty wall at the child's level. Tie a string in between the hooks. Let children clip their mittens on the line. Additionally, use these mittens for counting and matching. With a marker, write the same number on a pair of mittens. Drop all of the mittens in the middle of the table. Let children pair up the mittens by looking at the numbers on them.

Day #2

Art Activity

Winter Animals Collage: This is a group activity. Spread a large sheet of butcher paper on the floor. Provide children with glue and pictures of all kinds of winter animals (chipmunks, bears, snakes, turtles, frogs, squirrels, skunks, etc.). Let children spread the glue on the paper and place the pictures throughout the paper. If possible, include pictures of dens, burrows, etc. When the pictures have dried, display the collage on the wall at their eye level.

Circle Time

Establish a Circle Time routine. Read <u>The Hat</u> by Jan Brett. After finishing the story, pass around a clean stocking. Ask them to try it on as a hat. Does it fit? Is it expandable? Write their responses on chart paper.

Finger Play

Make copies of the images of the book, <u>The Hat</u>. Laminate and glue each of them to a craft stick. Use these pictures as props to retell the story.

Water Play

Add crushed ice to the water table. Provide children with shovels, measuring cups and winter animal figures. Ask children to wear mittens to protect their hands as they play with ice.

Squirrel Puzzle

Go for nature walk to look for squirrels and squirrel nets. Take a camera to take pictures of the squirrels eating, playing or crossing. Use the pictures taken during the squirrel hunt to make a puzzle. Mount the pictures on a colorful sheet of construction paper. Use different color construction paper for each picture. Laminate. Cut into puzzle pieces.

Math Activity

   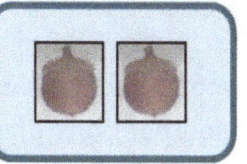

Picture by Maureen Ward, preschool teacher

<u>Math Cards</u>: Print out acorn pictures. Select five index cards. Write a number from one to five on the left side of each card. On the right side, attach and glue the number of acorns that matches the number on the card.

Sand Play

<u>Squirrel Habitat</u>: Substitute sand for dirt. Add small tree branches, leaves and plastic squirrels for creative play. Display pictures of squirrels in their homes. Let children use their imagination to create nests or dens for the squirrels.

Building with blocks

<u>Squirrel Habitat:</u> Let children create a squirrel home using building logs. Include logs of different lengths and wooden slats to create the den for ground squirrels or a nest for tree squirrels. Add plastic squirrels or laminated pictures of squirrels to the block area for more fun.

Game Play

<u>Ice Skating</u>: This activity can be done indoors or outdoors. Find an open area. Provide children with small boxes such as tissue boxes. If desired, children can decorate their boxes with stickers, crayons, markers or paint. Let children wear the boxes as if they were ice skates. Ask children to walk around the classroom or in the playground as if they were ice skating.

Day #3

Art Activity

Hockey Paint: For this activity, use a broomstick as a hockey stick and a small round wooden shape sorter as a puck. Tape a large sheet of butcher paper to the floor. Drop small portions of paint on the center of the paper. Place one child on one end of the paper and the other child on the other end. Help children push the "puck" from one side to the other until all paint colors are mixed.

Circle Time

Establish a Circle Time routine. Read <u>Froggy Gets Dressed</u> by Jonathan London. After reading the story, ask children to list all the pieces of clothing Froggy tried on and took off. Write their responses on chart paper.

Finger Play

Make an outline of Froggy out of cardboard. Enlarge and print pictures of the clothing Froggy wore: hats, mittens, boots, coat, hat, scarf, etc. Laminate. Glue Velcro pieces to the Froggy board and to Froggy's clothing. Help children dress and undress Froggy.

Water Play

Pour water in the water table. Add some small plastic animals, such as fish, turtles, and frogs. Make lily pads out of foam paper plates. Let children paint the plates with watercolors. Add the plates to the water and observe how the lily pads float while the watercolors start running and mixing into the water.

Music Time

Ask children to stand up in a circle. Sing and act out the following song.

I AM A LITTLE POLAR BEAR
Sung to the tune of "I'm a Little Teapot"

I'm a little polar bear
With white fur
My heavy coat
Keeps me warm
See me playing in the snow,
Cause' I never ever get cold!

Jacqueline Lopez

Sensory Play

Hare burrow: In a clear large plastic bowl, add potting soil, small toy animals, grass seed, small tree branches, leaves, measuring cups and spoons. Let children create dens and burrows for hares and other winter animals. Add water to the bowl regularly and watch the grassland grow.

Math Activity

Winter Clothes Chart: Make a chart of the clothes children wear on a winter day by writing the children's names and the items they wear next to their name. Attach a picture of the children wearing the clothing item (coat, scarf, boots, mittens, etc.) Let children comment on the differences.

Child's Name	Coat	Scarf	Boots	Mittens

Day #4

Art Activity

Winter Animal Stamping: Provide children with winter animal-shaped sponges or cookie cutters, glue, construction paper and paper plates. Pour glue on the paper plates. Dip the sponges or cookie cutters in the glue and press them on a piece of construction paper. When done printing, sprinkle with shimmering glitter.

Circle Time

Establish a Circle Time routine. Read <u>The Jacket I Wear in the Snow</u> by Shirley Neitzel. After reading the story, ask children to list all the pieces of clothing shown in the story and to list all pieces of clothing they wear on winter days. Write their responses on chart paper.

Finger Play

Make copies of the winter clothes shown in the story. Laminate and glue them to individual pieces of flannel. Using a flannel board, ask children to retell the story with the flannel props.

Water Play

Winter bottles: Use empty water bottles of different sizes for this activity. Help children add glitter, snowflake confetti and then water until the bottle is full. Place the cap on the bottle and seal with tape.

Movement

Scarf Dancing: Provide children with scarves. Play music and let the children swing, shake, and twirl the scarves as they dance.

Writing Center

Provide children with blue, white and black construction paper, ink pads of different colors and rubber stamps. Have children choose paper and a rubber stamp. Ask children to stamp designs all over the paper. For a shimmery finish, sprinkle glitter on the ink pads.

Water Play

Ice Fishing: Add crushed ice to the water table and cold water. Drop in plastic magnetic fish. Provide children with a fishing rod and let children catch the fish in the water. If magnetic fish are not available, make your own by printing fish pictures, laminating them and then attaching a piece of magnetic string to the back of the pictures. For the fishing rod, use a small stick, yarn and a piece of magnet at the end.

Dramatic Play

Add soft pillows and teddy bears to the dramatic area to create a "cave reading corner." Add books about winter, winter animals and outdoor winter clothing. If desired, you can tape pictures outside the tent of children engaged in different winter activities.

Writing Center

Add brown paper, bear stickers, bear cut-outs, markers and crayons, scissors and glue for children to decorate their winter scenery.

Day #5

 **Art Activity**

Iceberg Collage: Provide children with aluminum foil, petroleum jelly and wax paper. Let children tear a sheet of aluminum foil into different shapes. Give each child a sheet of wax paper. Let the children spread a dab of petroleum jelly all over the wax paper and then have the children place the pieces of aluminum foil one on top of the other to create an iceberg.

Circle Time

Establish a Circle Time routine. Read <u>I Can Ski</u> by Melanie Davis Jones and Terry Boles. After reading the story, ask children if they have ever gone skiing or seen somebody skiing. Can the children demonstrate the skiing basics, such as foot to foot and sliding side by side? Write their responses on chart paper.

Game Play

Paper Plate Skiing: Use paper plates as skis in order to engage children in physical activity. First, provide children with crayons and markers and let them personalize their own skis. Then let children stand on the paper plates and slide slowly as if they were skiing. As a safety precaution, ask two children to hold hands as they ski and remove all furniture to make more room.

Building with blocks
Provide children with blocks. Use the blocks to make a simple pattern on the floor. Have the children repeat and continue the pattern.

 ### Sensory Play
<u>Snow Dough:</u> Set up the table with flour, salt, water, vegetable oil and silver glitter. Let children make and knead the dough by mixing two cups of flour, one cup of salt and the glitter. Then add one cup of oil and one cup of water. Mix and knead well. Refrigerate in a Ziploc bag or airtight container.

Writing Center

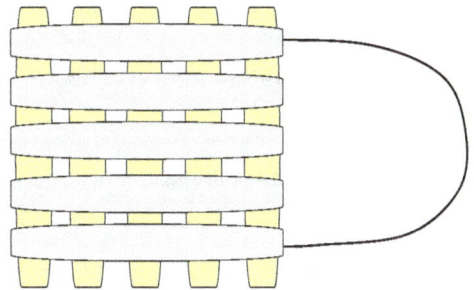

<u>Tongue Depressor Sled:</u> Provide children with tongue depressors, markers, and glue. Let children color the tongue depressors. Then ask children to place the tongue depressors in a row and glue another row of tongue depressors in the opposite direction. Attach a string on one side of the sled. Place small toys or toy figures on top of the sled and let children pull them around for sledding fun.

 ### Show and Tell
Ask children to bring to class photos or magazine pictures of winter animals, toys, winter clothes or anything that represents winter for Show and Tell.

PLANNING WEB
Week #4

Learning Center: **SOCIAL**	Learning Center: **MATH**	Learning Center: **LANGUAGE/BOOKS**	Group Time
- Ask children to describe their homes	- Use bear counters for counting and sorting	- <u>Bear Snores On</u> by Karma Wilson - <u>Don't Wake Up the Bear</u> by Marjorie Dennis Murray	<u>Small Group</u>: - Play the Hibernation Game <u>Large Group</u>: - Sing and act out "Grizzly Bears" song

Learning Center: **DRAMATIC PLAY**	**Developmental Goal:** - Instill togetherness and friendship among children by completing activities in groups - Involve children in winter-related activities **Story/Theme:** - <u>Time To Sleep</u> by Denise Fleming **Diversity:** - Display pictures of winter animals and their habitats		Routines/Transitions
- Create a bear cave out of a cardboard box			- <u>Letter Recognition</u>: Children will line up by stepping on their initials which are taped to the floor.

Learning Center: **ART/MUSIC/MOVEMENT**	**INDOORS OUTDOORS**	Health/Nutrition/Cooking	Learning Center: **SCIENCE/SENSORY**
- Make a cardboard bear cave. - Recite "Five Little Bears" - Create a train out of multiple shapes	<u>Indoors</u>: - Make a class book about hibernation. <u>Outdoors</u>: - "Go on a bear hunt" game	- Make "bear cupcakes" - Serve a rectangular snack	- Make "bear cookies" out of play-dough. - "Feely Box" activity

CLASS GOAL

Week #4

LEARN ABOUT HIBERNATION
AND
THE RECTANGLE SHAPE

Day #1

Art Activity

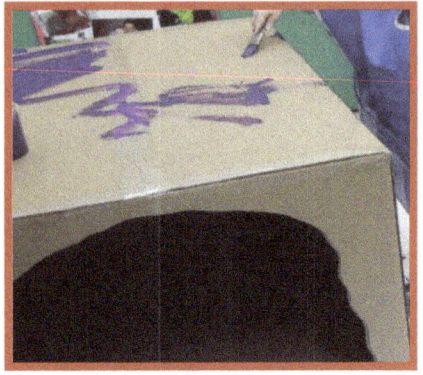

Bear Cave: Take a large box (big enough for children to play in) and cut an irregular opening in the front. Provide children with smocks, acrylic paint, and paintbrushes. Cover a wide area with old newspapers. Set the box on top. Let children paint the box brown or any other color they wish. Then glue scraps of green tissue paper on it to represent leaves.

Circle Time

Start Circle Time by gathering all children in a circle. Read Bear Snores On by Karma Wilson. Ask children to list all the animals who found their way to the bear's cave to keep warm. Ask children to share what they do when they feel cold. Do they snore in a cozy place? Write down their responses on chart paper.

Dramatic Play

Let the kids bring in teddy bears from home or add plastic bear toys to the dramatic play area. Allow the kids to recreate the hibernation process and display book pictures for guidance.

Math Activity

Provide children with bear counters and foam bowls. Paste a small construction paper circle in the middle of each bowl. Use red construction paper for red counters, blue paper for blue counters and so forth. Let children sort and count the bear counters in the bowls.

Finger Play

Recite the poem: "Five Little Bears." Make bear props to go along with the rhyme by gluing pictures of bears to a craft stick.

FIVE LITTLE BEARS

Five little bears went out to explore.
One left behind and then there were four.

Four little bears go on a shopping spree,
One went water-skiing and then there were three.

Three little bears had nothing to do,
One went sky-diving and that left two.

Two little bears were eating a honey bun,
One fell asleep and that left one.

One little bear sitting at dawn,
He felt all alone and ran home.

Jacqueline Lopez

Math Activity

Ask children to bring a teddy bear to school. Sort the bears according to size, color, etc. Children can also weigh the bears. Help children estimate who has the largest or smallest bear and/or who has the most lightweight or the heaviest one. Record their findings on chart paper.

Day #2

Art Activity

Sponge Painting Bears: For this project, use a bear paw sponge or make your own by cutting a bear paw shape out of a sponge and gluing pieces of sandpaper for claws. Provide children with coffee grounds, glue, water pitcher, and paper. Ask children to paint bear paws with watered down glue and then sprinkle coffee grounds on the prints.

Circle Time

Start Circle Time by gathering all children in a circle. Read Don't Wake Up the Bear by Marjorie Dennis Murray. Ask children to name other animals that sleep through the winter. Write down their responses on chart paper.

Game Play

Hibernation Activity Game: Make a hibernation game by printing pictures of bears and bear caves, beavers and beaver lodges, foxes and fox dens, squirrels and squirrel dreys, chipmunks and chipmunk burrows, skunks and skunk dens, etc. Make a chart by gluing pictures of all the animals. Cut out the pictures of the animal homes and help children match the animal with the corresponding home.

Snack Idea

Bear Cupcakes: Find a cupcake recipe and follow the directions. Before baking the cupcakes, insert a chocolate or cinnamon teddy graham cracker into each cupcake. The crackers do not melt during baking and the children get very excited to find the bear hidden in the cave cupcake.

Music Time

Gather all children in a circle. Help children learn the "Grizzly Bears" song for the next activity game.

GRIZZLY BEARS

Grizzly bears,
Oh grizzly bears,
Sleeping in your den.
Please be very quiet,
Very, very quiet.
If you shake him,
If you wake him,
He will growl at you!

Traditional

Game Play

Hibernation Game: Play a hibernation game. Select a child to be the bear. Ask the rest of the children to sit in a circle and then lie on the floor with their eyes closed. While everyone else sings "Grizzly Bears," ask the child selected to be the "bear" to walk around and to pick a child with a gentle shake. The "bear" selects another "bear" who wakes up with a growl and the game starts over. Continue until all children have a turn.

Writing Center

Staple several white pages to make a book. Use any colored paper as a book cover. Provide children with bear stencils, markers and crayons. Give children time to trace and decorate their bears. Add pom-poms, stickers, scraps of paper, and glitter.

Day #3

Art Activity

Bear Prints: Set up the art table with white crayons, sandpaper, and watercolor paints. Cut bear shapes out of sandpaper. Tape the cutouts to the table. Have each child take a piece of paper and place it on top of the bear shape. Tape this paper to the table so it doesn't slide. Help the children use the side of the crayon to rub firmly over the design. Then let them put watercolor on the paper using a thin brush until the bear design appears.

Circle Time

Establish a Circle Time routine. Read <u>Time To Sleep</u> by Denise Fleming. Ask children to recall the animals that hibernate during wintertime. Write down their responses on chart paper.

Writing Center

Make a class book about bears. If possible, include pictures of all eight kind of bears: American black bears, polar bears, giant panda bears, Asiatic black bears, sloth bears, spectacled bears, sun bears and brown bears which are also known as grizzly bears. Also, include art work of children and pictures of children holding their teddy bears or playing in the bear cave. Lastly, include information about bears: What do they eat? Where do they live? Laminate the pictures. Punch two holes and display the book in the reading corner.

Math Activity

Bear Growth Chart: Make a growth chart to compare the size of a bear with the height of each child. Draw the head of a bear and place it above the chart. Tape the chart to an empty wall. Record the children's height on a chart. Record their height periodically to see if children have grown. Write any changes on the board and record the date as well.

Child's Name	Height

Science Activity

Bear fur provides excellent insulation from the cold just like winter coats, scarves, and mittens protect us. To help children understand this concept, ask children to wear their coats and mittens to play in the snow (or use ice cubes). Encourage children to hold snow with both hands wearing only one mitten. Ask children to observe how the hand that is covered is warm while the other hand is cold and red. Explain children that bear fur is like the mittens that keep their bodies warm and cozy during winter days.

Day #4

Art Activity

<u>Rectangle Collage:</u> Set up the art table with a large sheet of butcher paper, glue, and paintbrushes. Cut rectangle shapes out of construction paper, tissue paper, wallpaper, felt, etc. Ask children to brush glue on the paper. Then let them place the rectangular cutouts on the paper.

Circle Time

Establish a Circle Time routine. Read <u>We're Going On A Bear Hunt</u> by Michael Rosen. Ask children if they have ever gone on family outings like hiking or fishing. What experiences can they recall from that adventure? Write down their responses on chart paper.

Movement

Play "We're Going On A Bear Hunt" song or sing along with the children. Provide children with hats, binoculars, dress up clothing and invite them to a fantasy bear hunt. Act out this interactive story and take the class on an imaginary adventure by performing various actions and sounds to mimic the events in the journey.

Building with blocks

Invite children to gather around the Lego table. Ask children to find all colorful rectangular Lego blocks and store all other blocks. Encourage children to build different structures using the rectangular blocks.

Snack Idea

Have a rectangular snack. Use a rectangular cookie-cutter to cut a rectangle out of a loaf of bread; cut square slices of cheese in half to make two rectangles. Cut rectangular sheets of paper as placemats and pass out the bread and the cheese on previously cut rectangular paper plates. Also serve juice boxes as drinks.

Writing Center

Draw the shape of a rectangle on a piece of paper. Provide children with yarn, glue, markers or crayons. Encourage children to color the rectangle. Then add glue to the rectangle outline to place the yarn on top.

Game Play

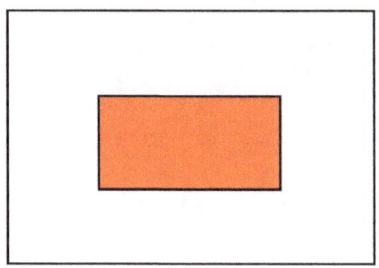 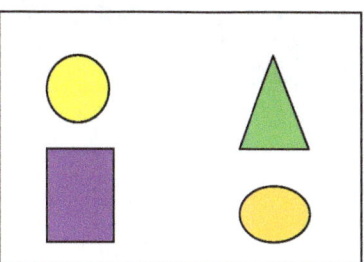

Rectangle Shape Hunt: For this activity, set up two tables in the class: one with a big rectangle shape taped in the middle and the other one with different shapes taped on it. Ask the children to look for and find all rectangle-shaped items and place them on the rectangle table. If they bring any item that does not have a rectangle shape, help them place the items correctly on the other table. At the end, have them count how many rectangle items they found.

Sand Play

Treasure Rectangle Hunt: Hide in the bottom of the sand table as many rectangle items that children are familiar with and that are part of the class. Let children scoop the sand out to find the hidden treasure.

Show and Tell

Ask children to bring in to school different items that they have at home that have a rectangular shape. Help them present their findings during Show and Tell in class.

Day #5

 **Art Activity**

<u>**Multiple Shape Train:**</u> Trace and cut different sheets of construction paper to form this shape train. Cover the art table with old newspapers. Provide children with smocks, spoons, paints of different colors and golf balls. Pair up children face to face and side by side. Place scoops of paints of two or three colors on the middle of the paper. Let children roll the golf balls back and forth to mix all colors and form different patterns. Repeat the same procedure until all shapes are colored to complete the train. Have the children name all the other shapes they see. Dry and display on an empty wall.

Circle Time

Establish a Circle Time routine. Read <u>The Shape Of Things</u> by Julie Lacome. Ask children to recognize the different shapes around the classroom. Help children understand that common objects around us are made of shapes. Point out the clock, the table, and the cabinets and see if they can identify the shapes. Then divide children in groups of three or four. Provide each group with a bag of shapes of different colors and sizes. Ask children to work together to create anything they want using these shapes. Be prepared to assist younger players. Write down their responses on chart paper.

Sensory Play

Feely Box: Place different items brought from home (toy, notebook, etc.) or found in the classroom inside a feely box. Let the children close their eyes and put their hands in to take out an item. Encourage the child to describe the shape of the item and then to try to identify it. Make sure to include questions like: How many sides does your item have? Does it have bumpy sides? What do you think it is?

Music Time

Cut rectangles out of construction paper and glue them to craft sticks to use as props for the following song.

RECTANGLE IS ITS NAME
Sung to the tune of: "London Bridge is Falling Down"

I know a shape
That has four sides
Two are long
And two are short.

I know a shape
That is like this
And rectangle is its name!

Jacqueline Lopez

Game Play

Hopscotch Shape Play: This activity can be played outdoors or indoors. Use crayons of different colors to draw different shapes for hopscotch play. Number each shape for an extended learning experience. Help children jump from shape to shape and name each shape.

February

Health

Parent Letter
FEBRUARY NEWS

Dear Parents,

This month we are going to start a new unit devoted to Health. During this month we will discuss healthy foods, healthy habits and healthy fitness. We are also going to dedicate one segment to the five senses and how we use them in everyday activities. Kids who learn healthy eating and exercise habits early in life carry those habits into adulthood. Parents can set an example by drinking water instead of sweetened beverages. Fostering healthy habits can save children from developing chronic diseases.

Children are going to be involved in diverse activities to develop an understanding and awareness of nutrition. It is essential for a child to maintain a healthy weight. Also, good nutrition helps children concentrate more in school. A well-balanced diet combined with daily physical activities helps children keep their bodies healthy.

We are going to divide this unit into four small segments to help the children acquire a good understanding of:

- Doctor and Dentist visits
- Healthy Habits
- Nutrition
- The Five Senses

Some of the activities planned for this month include:

- Creating a healthy food collage
- Eating healthy snacks
- Weighing and measuring our bodies
- Creating a bumpy wall

We look forward to working on this theme and learning more important facts about health.

PLANNING WEB
Week #1

Learning Center: SOCIAL
- Have children talk about their experiences during their visits to the doctor

Learning Center: MATH
- Make a height and weight chart
- Make an eye color chart

Learning Center: LANGUAGE/BOOKS
- Froggy Goes To The Doctor by Jonathan London
- I Am Growing by Aliki

Group Time

Small Group:
- Make X-Ray drawings

Large Group:
- Sing and act out "Brush your teeth" by Raffi

Learning Center: DRAMATIC PLAY
- Turn the dramatic play area into an examination room. Add cots, dolls, bandages, etc to the area

Developmental Goal:
- Encourage children to participate in daily chores
- Encourage children to continue copying positive adult behavior and activities

Story/Theme:
- Visiting The Doctor by DK Publishing

Diversity:
- Display pictures of stretchers and other hospital equipment around the classroom

Routines/Transitions

Stop the Germs Routine:
- Show children how to cover their sneezes and coughs to avoid spreading germs

Learning Center: ART/MUSIC/MOVEMENT
- Band-aids collage
- Glove painting
- Dental floss painting
- "I wonder if I'm growing," song
- "Miss Polly had a dolly" rhyme

INDOORS OUTDOORS

Indoors:
- Play with band-aids number chart

Outdoors:
- Draw a tooth-shaped hopscotch with chalk

Health/Nutrition/Cooking
- Show children the proper tooth brushing procedure

Snack Idea:
- Serve a "big smile" for snack

Learning Center: SCIENCE/SENSORY
- Add empty, clean cold medicine bottles, eye droppers, empty hand soap bottles, spray bottles, and liquid soap to the water table

CLASS GOAL

Week #1

**STAY HEALTHY:
VISITS TO DOCTORS AND DENTISTS**

Day #1

Art Activity

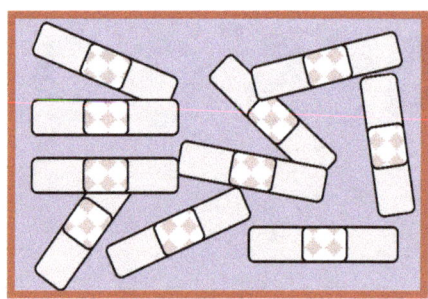

Band-Aid Art: Set up the art table with band-aids and construction paper. Let children place the band-aids on the paper to make a collage.

Circle Time
Start Circle Time by gathering all children in a circle. Read <u>Froggy Goes To The Doctor</u> by Jonathan London. Ask children to describe what doctors do when children go for a check-up. Write their responses on chart paper.

Dramatic Play
Turn the dramatic play area into an examination room. Use a child's cot as doctor's bed. Add blankets, notepads, markers, vest, play phone and doctor's tools: bandages, gauze, stethoscope, and a doctor's bag. Ask children to take turns pretending to be the patient and the doctor.

Water Play
Add empty, clean cold medicine bottles, eye droppers, empty hand soap bottles, spray bottles, and liquid soap to the water table. Let children fill the containers while talking about each object's use.

Math Activity

Eye Color Chart: Make an eye color chart. Observe and record the number of children who have brown, black, hazel, blue or green eyes. Graph the results by taking pictures of the children's eye color and placing them in the corresponding column. Ask children to count how many children in the class have the same eye color. Which one is the predominant eye color?

Child's Name	👁	👁	👁	👁

Game Play

Band-Aids Number Chart: Make a number chart using band-aids. Stick band-aids to a piece of construction paper. Cut and laminate. Add a piece of Velcro to the back of the band-aid cards. Place the correct number of cards next to the corresponding number on the chart.

1	🩹
2	🩹🩹
3	🩹🩹🩹
4	🩹🩹🩹🩹
5	🩹🩹🩹🩹🩹

Day #2

Art Activity

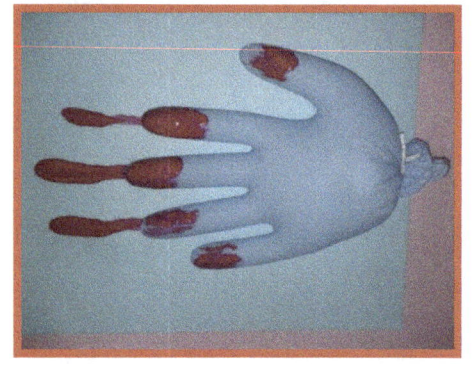

Glove Painting: Set up the art table with paint trays of different colors, surgical gloves, construction paper and a cup of water. Let children examine the gloves. Then, fill the gloves with water and tie a knot. Let children dip the water gloves in the paint and rub them on the paper to make a design.

Circle Time

Start Circle Time by gathering all children in a circle. Read I'm Growing by Aliki. Ask children to describe what doctors do when children go for a check-up. Write their responses on chart paper.

Writing Center

X-Ray Art: Add black construction paper, bone stickers, white chalk and silver glitter. Let children place the stickers on the paper and decorate it with the glitter and chalk to make unique x-ray pictures.

Building with blocks

Display pictures of hospital stretchers near the block area. Provide children with different types of blocks and people figurines. Let children use their imaginations to create beddings for their figurines.

Finger Play

Let children sit in a circle holding a doll or teddy bear to recite the following rhyme:

MISS LULU HAD A DOLL

Miss Lulu had a doll
Doll, doll
Who was dressed for a walk,
Walk, walk.
She put the doll in the stroller,
Stroller, stroller
And they walked a block,
Block, block

Jacqueline Lopez

Body Puzzle

Place paper large enough to trace a child's entire body on the floor. Cut out the child's outline and glue it to poster board. Divide the picture into puzzle pieces. The bigger the pieces, the easier it will be for the children to handle them. Glue the individual pieces to a colorful sheet of construction paper. Laminate. Let the children put the pieces together over a carpet. For extra fun, take individual pictures of boys and girls and go over the differences in appearance, such as height, weight, hair color, clothing, etc.

Reflection

Describe children's growth and how the different parts of the body change. Ask children if they know the emergency number.

Day #3

Art Activity

Syringe Painting: Instruct children to wear smocks and help cover the art area with old newspapers. Set up the art area with a large piece of butcher paper, paint cups, large needle-less syringes and tape. Secure the paper to an empty wall with tape. Let children stand three to four feet from the paper. Help children absorb the paint from the paint cup with the syringe and spray the paint onto the paper to make a design.

Circle Time

Start Circle Time by gathering all children in a circle. Read Visiting The Doctor by DK Publishing. Ask children to describe their favorite part of the story. Do they feel nervous when they visit the doctor? Write their responses on chart paper.

Math Activity

Height Chart: Measure and record each child's height. Then make footprints of each child with paint, overlapping one another until the child's height is reached. Make a weight chart as well and place it next to the height chart.

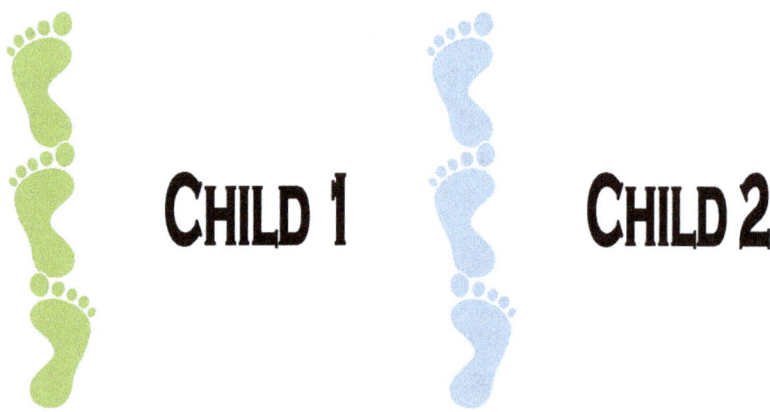

Music Time

Sit down in a circle to sing the following song by Raffi:

I WONDER IF I AM GROWING

I Wonder if I am growing
I Wonder if I am growing
My mom says yes I am growing
But it is hard for me to see
My mom says eat your sandwich
It will make you grow up tall
But when I eat my sandwich
I am hardly bigger at all

And I wonder if I am growing
I wonder if I am growing
My mom says yes I am growing
But it is hard for me to see
My mom says wash your hands now
Then you can go and play
Hey! I can reach the tap now
For the very first time today.
And I think I must be growing
Oh I know I am really growing
My <u>mom</u> says yes I am growing
And now I know it is true.

Raffi

Day #4

 **Art Activity**

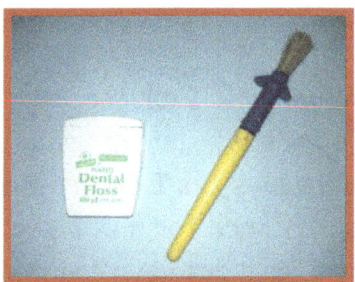

Dental Floss Painting: Provide children with paper, paints of different colors, paper plates, and dental floss. Make different paint trays by pouring each paint color on different plates. Have children dip a piece of dental floss into the paint and then move it around the paper to make a design.

Circle Time
Start Circle Time by gathering all children in a circle. Read <u>Does A Tiger Open Wide?</u> by Fred Ehrlich. Ask children to recall the last time they visited the dentist. Have them each share one thing that will happen when they visit the dentist. Write their responses on chart paper.

Sensory Play
Provide each child with toothpaste and a Ziploc bag. Help children squeeze the paste into the bag. Seal the bag with tape. Allow children to play and feel the paste texture.

 **Water Play**
Set up the water table with soap and water. Include plastic toys and toothbrushes. Let children wash the toys with the toothbrushes.

Building with blocks
Set up the block area with medium-sized Lego blocks. Cut pieces of aluminum foil. Let children cover the blocks with the foil to pretend to make fillings.

Game Play

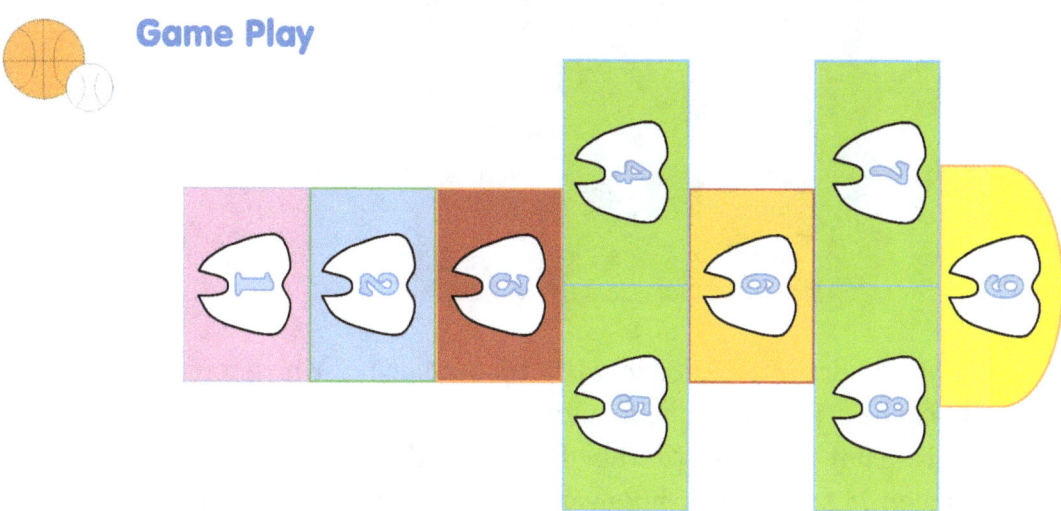

<u>Tooth-Shaped Hopscotch:</u> Set up an outdoor area. Make a tooth-shaped hopscotch by drawing teeth shapes with chalk.

 **Resource People**
Invite a dental hygienist to visit the school.

 **Reflection**
How often should children brush their teeth?
What kinds of foods contain calcium?
How often should children visit a dentist?
What can contribute to tooth cavities or decay?

Day #5

 **Art Activity**

Painting with Toothbrushes: Provide children with food coloring, white tempera paint, paint trays and toothbrushes. Make individual trays for each paint color used. Ask children to mix the white paint with the toothbrush and add two or three drops of red food coloring. Ask children to spread the mix over the paper to make designs.

Circle Time

Start Circle Time by gathering all children in a circle. Read <u>You Think It's Easy Being The Tooth Fairy?</u> by Sheri Bell-Rehwoldt. Ask children to describe their favorite part of the story. Write their responses on chart paper.

Snack Idea

Gather the following ingredients to make a "big smile" snack: loaf of bread, circle-shaped cookie cutter, cream cheese, red food coloring and small marshmallow chunks. Let children cut the bread using the cookie cutter. Add two or three drops of food coloring to the cream cheese. Mix well. Spread the cream cheese on the bread. Place the marshmallows on the edge of the circle to represent the teeth. Fold the bread. Serve with milk.

Sand Play
For this activity, fill the sand table with sand. Place white Unifix blocks deep inside the sand. Let children dig in the sand to find "the missing teeth."

Writing Center
Make a tooth shape from a piece of sandpaper. Tape it to the table. Let children put a sheet of paper on top of the shape. Use the side of the crayon to rub over the shape until the shape appears.

Movement
Divide the class in two small groups. Let one group be the "toothbrushes" and the other group be the "teeth." Let the groups stand in rows facing each other. The idea is that the toothbrushes will try to reach the teeth to keep them clean. Let the "toothbrushes" move *forward* dancing, jumping, skipping or hopping to reach the "teeth," which will move *backwards* to avoid being "brushed." Play the activity as long as interest lasts.

Show and Tell
Ask children to bring in new toothbrushes and small toothpaste tubes. Let them explain to the class the color of toothbrushes they brought, what type of toothpaste flavor they have, etc. In small groups, model how to properly brush your teeth. Allow time for children to brush their teeth and provide a small cup of water to rinse.

Reflection
Why is it important to keep our teeth healthy?
How can we avoid bad breath?

PLANNING WEB
Week #2

Learning Center: SOCIAL - Have children sit in a circle to discuss healthy habits	**Learning Center: MATH** - <u>Hand-washing chart</u>: Take pictures of children following hand-washing procedure.	**Learning Center: LANGUAGE/BOOKS** - <u>I Love Bathtime</u> by Joy Berry - <u>Brush Your Teeth Please Pop-Up</u> by Leslie McGuire - <u>I Am Not Sleepy</u> by Jonathan Allen	**Group Time** **Small Group:** - Make a picture book about hand-washing **Large Group:** - Have a "Pajama Party"
Learning Center: DRAMATIC PLAY - Set up the dramatic play area as a dental office	**Developmental Goal:** - Encourage children to use language by naming things they see and touch instead of pointing at them - Praise children for routine hand washing **Story/Theme:** - <u>Wash Your Hands</u> by Tony Ross **Diversity:** - Display pictures of children's healthy habits		**Routines/Transitions** **Stop the Germs Game:** - Show how children spread germs by simply spraying colored water on paper every time a child pretends to sneeze or cough
Learning Center: ART/MUSIC/MOVEMENT - Bubble bath prints - Handprint germs - Decorate pillowcases - "Take a bath everyday" song - "Brush Your Teeth" song	**INDOORS OUTDOORS** <u>Indoors</u>: - Make fitness flash cards <u>Outdoors</u>: - Trip to the park	**Health/Nutrition/Cooking** - Wash and scrub baby dolls with soap and water <u>Snack Idea</u>: - Serve a healthy snack	**Learning Center: SCIENCE/SENSORY** - Display bar soap products for children to see and touch - Teeth stain activity

CLASS GOAL

Week #2

HELP CHILDREN
DEVELOP HEALTHY HABITS

Day #1

 **Art Activity**

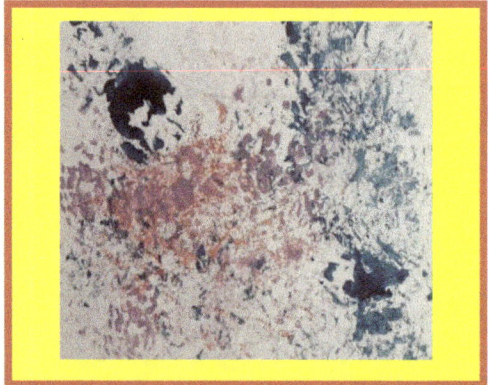

Bubble Bath Prints: Set up the art table with baby bath solution, rubber bath toys, sponges, straw, bubble wand, light color construction paper, paint trays (*use at least two bright tempera paint colors*) and a container full of water. Add the bath solution to the water until it becomes a soapy solution. Blow bubbles using the straws and the bubble wand. Dip the sponges or the rubber toys in the paint and print on the paper. Then set the paper over the bubbles and hold it in place until several bubbles have popped and have transferred their shapes to the paper to make a print.

 **Circle Time**

Start Circle Time by gathering all children in a circle. Read <u>I Love Bathtime</u> by Joy Berry. Ask children to name toys they use during bath time. Do they use bubble wash or soap? Write their responses on chart paper.

Science Activity

Add different kinds of bar soaps, soap flakes in a tight container, soap solution and a magnifying glass to the science area.

Water Play

Pour baby gel solution to the water table. Add plastic dolls, bath sponges and wash cloths. Ask children to bathe the dolls and scrub them clean. Dry them with a towel.

Music Time

Sit children in a circle to sing the following song.

TAKE A BATH EVERYDAY
Sung to "Happy Birthday!"

Take a bath everyday,
And keep dirt away
From head to toes
Bath time is the way!

Jacqueline Lopez

Magnetic Body Puzzle

Take pictures of the children standing up. Print them out on letter-sized paper. Glue each picture to different sheets of color construction paper. Laminate all pictures. Cut out the pictures to make puzzle pieces. If desired, laminate the pictures again for continued use. Let children put the puzzle pieces together.

Reflection

Review how and why we take baths.
Can children name their body parts?
What are other ways we can take good care of our bodies?

Day #2

Art Activity

Healthy Smile Collage: Provide children with old magazines, glue and paper. Encourage children to cut or tear pictures of people smiling. Brush glue over the paper and let children arrange the pictures as they wish. When the pictures have dried, display the collage on the wall.

Circle Time

Start Circle Time by gathering all children in a circle. Read <u>Brush Your Teeth Please Pop-Up</u> by Leslie McGuire. Ask children to share how often they brush their teeth. What is their favorite toothpaste? Write their responses on chart paper.

Science Activity

Teeth Stain Activity: To demonstrate how sugar foods can cause cavities if the food is not removed properly with brushing, leave hard-boiled eggs overnight in a bowl of coke in the fridge. The next day, put the stained hard-boiled eggs in a bathroom cup, provide children with brushes and encourage them to "brush the stain off."

Dramatic Play

Set up the dramatic play area as a dental office. Include smocks, toothbrushes, small chairs for the examination and waiting rooms, baby dolls, empty mouthwash bottles, toothpaste, notebooks, crayons and markers, trays for tools, and sheets of paper towels. Ask children to sit the dolls in chairs and cover their clothes with the towel to pretend to be dentists checking the teeth of their "patients."

Snack Idea

Prepare a delicious, healthy snack for children. Include fruit slices, vegetable sticks, milk or water as a drink.

Music Time

Sing along and act out a song written and sung by Raffi.

BRUSH YOUR TEETH

When you wake up in the morning, it's quarter to one
And you want to have a little fun
You brush your teeth, ch ch ch ch, ch ch ch ch
You brush your teeth, ch ch ch ch, ch ch ch ch

When you wake up in the morning, it's quarter to two
And you want to find something to do
You brush your teeth, ch ch ch ch, ch ch ch ch
You brush your teeth, ch ch ch ch, ch ch ch ch

And when you wake up in the morning, it's quarter to three
And your mind starts hummin' tweedle dee dee
You brush your teeth, ch ch ch ch, ch ch ch ch
You brush your teeth, ch ch ch ch, ch ch ch ch

When you wake up in the morning, it's quarter to four
And you think you hear a knock on your door
You brush your teeth, ch ch ch ch, ch ch ch ch
You brush your teeth, ch ch ch ch, ch ch ch ch

When you wake up in the morning, it's quarter to five
And you just can't wait to come alive
You brush your teeth, ch ch ch ch, ch ch ch ch
You brush your teeth, ch ch ch ch, ch ch ch ch
You brush your teeth, ch ch ch ch, ch ch ch ch

Day #3

Art Activity

Hand-Printing Germs: Set up the art table. Include dark colored finger-paints and paper. Place a small amount of finger-paint on a section of the table. Use at least two or three different colors. Ask children to spread the paint on their hands and then press them on the paper. Repeat this with the other paints. Encourage children to observe how the paint colors are mixed. Notice that the last prints are even darker than the original ones (germ stains).

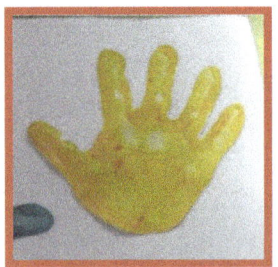

Circle Time

Start Circle Time by gathering all children in a circle. Read <u>Wash Your Hands</u> by Tony Ross. Ask children questions about the story. What was their favorite part? Listen to their responses while you prepare for the following activity. Put a dab of glitter on your hands and "touch the children's hands." Discuss how only soap and water can get rid of the germs. Ask some of the children to rub and try to wipe the germs (glitter) off their hands while others wash their hands with soap and water. Ask children to observe and compare the results. Write their responses on chart paper.

Sand Play

Add glitter and sand tools to the sand table. Moisten the sand. Ask children to play and mold the sand using their hands. When children are done, remind them to wash their hands.

Writing Center

Take pictures of children in different activities (painting, playing, etc.) and of children washing their hands afterwards. Glue, laminate and make a picture book.

Game Play

Add food coloring to a spray water bottle. Tape a large piece of white construction paper to an empty wall. Ask children to pretend they are sneezing or coughing in front of the paper. Each time the child sneezes or coughs, spray the water bottle and ask them to observe how "germs" spread and leave a trace when we don't cover our mouths and noses.

Water Play

Have children put their smocks on and gather around the water table. Add soap and plastic toys. Ask children to wash and rinse the toys. Let them air dry.

Math Activity

Hand-washing Number Cards: Make hand-washing number cards. Take pictures of children following step by step the hand-washing procedure:

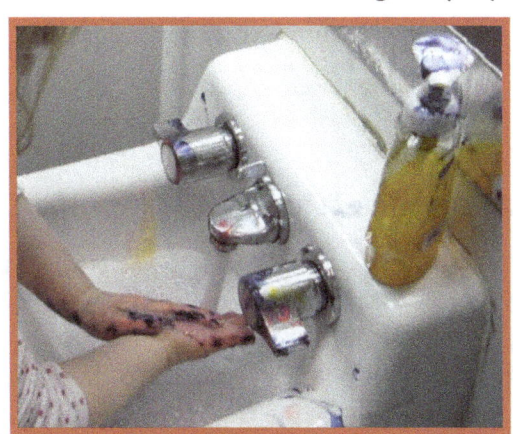

1) Use soap and running water;
2) Rub hands back and forth and in between fingers;
3) Rinse;
4) Dry hands with paper towel;
5) Turn off faucet with paper towel and discard it in the waste basket.

Laminate the cards. Let children find the right sequence.

Day #4

Art Activity

Bouncing Ball Prints: Set up the art table with paints of different colors and small balls. Ask children to dip the balls in the paint and bounce or roll them on the paper to make a print. Repeat these steps with all paints.

Circle Time

Start Circle Time by gathering all children in a circle. Read From Head To Toe by Eric Carle. Ask children to describe their favorite part of the story. Then review all of the things the children in the story were able to do and act out these movements with the children. Provide children time to repeat all movements. Write their responses on a chart paper.

Game Play

Set up an outdoor area for children to play. Have different fitness activities for children prepared: hula hoop rings, toss and ring activities, hopscotch, obstacle course, etc. Encourage children to try each one of the activities planned and observe how they run, skip, gallop and move from one activity to another.

Movement

Play a music CD. Ask children to dance to the beat of the music by moving their upper and lower body.

Resource People

Invite a gym trainer or an aerobic instructor to visit the school and talk to the children about their occupation.

Building with blocks

Spread blocks on a carpeted area. Ask children to sit or kneel to build different structures.

Math Activity

Fitness Activity Flash Cards: Make fitness activity cards. Include pictures of children doing different activities: jumping jacks, kicking or tossing balls, swimming, playing basketball, walking, etc., and number each card.

Field Trip

Trip to the Park: Take the children for a walk to the park and take a ball with you. Encourage children to bounce and kick the ball to one another, climb on the playground equipment or simply let children run in the field.

Water Play

Set up an area for water play. Fill a bucket with water. Add water toys and measuring cups for a fun-filled activity.

Game Play

Parachute Play: This activity can be done on the playground or in the park as well. Set out the parachute in a wide empty space. Remove furniture if needed. Ask children to stand around it in a circle. Encourage children to turn their bodies sideways and hold the parachute with one hand as they walk in a circle, reminding them to watch where they are going to avoid falls. Sing "Ring around the Rosie..." and ask children to walk, hop, skip, jump, etc.

Reflection

What are some fitness activities that build children's strength and endurance? How can sports benefit children?
What are the children's favorite outdoor activities?
Do they play sports with their parents?

Day #5

Art Activity

Decorating pillowcases: Cover the art table with old newspapers. Encourage children to wear aprons. Provide children with fabric paints of different colors, pre-washed pillowcases, sponges of different shapes, and trays. Set up paint trays with sponges. Let children dip the sponge in the paint and press it on the pillowcase to make a print. Let one side of the pillowcase dry before painting the other side.

Circle Time

Start Circle Time by gathering all children in a circle. Read I Am Not Sleepy by Jonathan Allen. Ask children what they do to avoid bedtime. What is their sleep routine? Write their responses on chart paper.

Dramatic Play

Place a tent in the dramatic play area or make your own by covering adult chairs with a throw. Include camping gear such as flashlights, backpacks, blankets, sleeping bags, pillows, etc.

Show and Tell

Pajama Party: Arrange a pajama day. Have children come in pajamas for the day with their teddy bears and favorite nighttime stories. Play nighttime music and encourage children to share or read a book to one another. Ask children to discuss with their friends their nighttime routine at home.

Writing Center

Decorating slippers: Ask children to take their shoes off. Provide children with paper, construction paper, stickers, markers, crayons, scissors, and pencils. Encourage (or help them if needed) children to trace their own feet on the paper. Assist children in cutting out their feet shape. Let children decorate their "slippers" as they wish.

 ### Movement
Play a lullaby CD. Turn the light off. Have children pretend to sleep while the song plays and then "wake up" when the lights are on and the music stops.

 ### Writing Center

Add star stickers and black construction paper to the writing center. Ask children to decorate the paper with the stickers.

 ### Snack Idea
Serve a naptime snack. Provide children with apple slices, diced oranges, vegetable sticks, water and milk.

 ### Building with blocks
Set up the block area inside a tent. Include animals and people figurines for more fun.

 ### Reflection
How can children benefit from a daily naptime routine?
What can you do with children who avoid napping?
What can you do with children who are afraid of the dark?

PLANNING WEB
Week #3

Learning Center: SOCIAL - Ask children about the importance of eating healthy	**Learning Center: MATH** - Sort fruits and vegetables	**Learning Center: LANGUAGE/BOOKS** - <u>What Am I?: Looking Through Shapes at Apples and Grapes</u> by N. N. Charles	**Group Time** **Small Group:** - Make a color board game **Large Group:** - Taste test activity. - Memory card game
Learning Center: DRAMATIC PLAY - Turn the dramatic play area into a restaurant	**Developmental Goal:** - Encourage children to use their imagination to play - Encourage slow-to-warm-up children and energetic children to sit and play together. Observe their interaction **Story/Theme:** - <u>The Very Hungry Caterpillar</u> by Eric Carle **Diversity:** - Display pictures of healthy foods from different countries		**Routines/Transitions** **Healthy Path:** - Number healthy food, that is, one for apple, two for carrots, etc. Laminate and tape to the floor. Ask children to step on the pictures to move from one activity to another
Learning Center: ART/MUSIC/MOVEMENT - Fruits and vegetable prints. - Kitchen gadget prints. - Healthy food placemats - "My own plate" rhyme	**INDOORS OUTDOORS** **Indoors:** - Make a picture book of fruits and vegetables **Outdoors:** - Trip to the Grocery Store	**Health/Nutrition/Cooking** - Make a chart of "healthy" and "unhealthy" snacks **Snack Idea:** - Serve a healthy fruit snack	**Learning Center: SCIENCE/SENSORY** - Add cornmeal to the sensory table - Make play-dough

CLASS GOAL

Week #3

DEVELOP HEALTHY
EATING HABITS

Day #1

Art Activity

Fruit and vegetable prints: Set up the art table with paints of different colors, construction paper, fruits and vegetables. For better handling, cut fruits like oranges and apples in half and insert a fork for children to use as a handle. Let children dip the fruits or vegetables in the paint to make a print. Consider using different paint colors for each food used.

Circle Time

Start Circle Time by gathering all children in a circle. Read <u>The Very Hungry Caterpillar</u> by Eric Carle. Ask children to share their favorite food to eat. List all their choices on a chart.

Finger Play

Reproduce the pictures of the fruits and vegetables the caterpillar ate. Laminate and glue them to a piece of felt. Attach a Velcro piece to the back of the felt. Make an egg, little and big caterpillar, a cocoon, and a butterfly out of felt. Allow children to retell the story using these pieces.

Dramatic Play

Turn the dramatic play area into a restaurant. Include menus with pictures of dinners, fruits and vegetables from old magazines, pots and pans, play food, tablecloth, plates, utensils, napkins and kitchen vests or aprons. Encourage children to take turns being the waitress or waiter, cook and customer.

Writing Center

Collect food magazines from local grocery stores. Provide children with scissors, glue and paper. Help children tear or cut the pictures out and glue them to construction paper. When done, turn it into a book for parents and children to see.

Math Activity
Fruits and vegetables sorting activity: Prepare this activity to help children learn the difference between fruits and vegetables.

Make color-coded pictures of vegetables and fruits to help children sort food. Copy pictures of fruits and paste them on green construction paper; copy pictures of vegetables and paste them on yellow construction paper. Attach a piece of Velcro to the back of each picture. Let children stick the pictures to the corresponding green or yellow board.

Game Play

Color board game: Laminate sheets of color construction paper (*red for apples, strawberries; green for peppers, cucumbers, etc.*) Attach magnetic strips to the laminated paper. Cut fruits and vegetables from food magazines and laminate them. Cut and glue magnetic strips to the back of each object. Use magnetic boards and let children arrange the fruits and vegetables by color.

 **Reflection**
What kinds of food keep us healthy?
How do you know a vegetable from a fruit?

Day #2

Art Activity

Kitchen gadget prints: Provide children with construction paper and plastic kitchen tools such as spoons, potato mashers, whisks, forks, etc. For better results, use play kitchen tools since they are smaller and easier to handle for the small hands of children. Set up painting trays of different colors. Let children dip each tool in different color paints and make a print on the paper. While doing this activity, ask children to name the tool and its use.

Circle Time

Start Circle Time by gathering all children in a circle. Read What Am I?: Looking Through Shapes at Apples and Grapes by N. N. Charles. Ask children to describe their favorite part of the story. Can they think of all of the food shown in the book? What shapes were used to make the fruit or vegetable? Write their responses on chart paper.

Sensory Play

Taste Test Activity: For this activity, pick two or three children that are willing to participate in a taste test. Cut fruits in different sizes. Blindfold the children. On a paper plate, put one slice of fruit in front of the children. Let them touch or smell to guess the fruit. While they are involved in this activity, ask the children to describe the shape and taste of the fruit. Ask questions such as: Is it sweet or sour? Does it have seeds?

Snack Idea

Serve a nutritious snack. Give each child a paper plate. Cut different fruits such as apples, grapes, kiwi, banana, etc. If possible, cut the fruit into different shapes. Place each cut fruit in different plates. Allow children to select the fruit they like and then use their imagination to make any designs they wish on their plate. Let them show their creations before they eat them.

Finger Play

Help children recite and act out this rhyme:

MY OWN PYRAMID PLATE

I made my own plate
With four groups:
One is a slice of bread,
Two are some chunks of fruits;
Three includes my favorite beans;
Four is a piece of meat
That I must eat
If I want to grow big.
For drink there is not better choice
Than a glass of milk
What a thrill!

Jacqueline Lopez

Building with blocks

Add Lego people, a barn, tractor and animals, and play vegetables for children to play and pretend to be farmers.

Sand Play

Add cornmeal to the sensory table. Provide children with measuring cups, play shovels and other tools used for planting.

Field Trip

Plan a trip to a nearby grocery store for children to see all kinds of fruits and vegetables, grains, meat and poultry.

Day #3

Art Activity

Healthy Food Placemats: Cut out a large white circle. Provide children with sheets of color construction paper, food magazines, and glue. Let children tear or cut their favorite food and paste it on the circle. Include a picture of the child eating his/her favorite meal. Then glue the circle to the center of the construction paper. Paste a picture of a spoon, fork and a small circle for a cup. Laminate.

Circle Time

Start Circle Time by gathering all children in a circle. Read <u>If You Give a Moose a Muffin</u> by Laura Joffe Numeroff. Ask children to recall all the things the moose did and ate. What was their favorite part of the story? Write their responses on chart paper.

Math Activity

HEALTHY ✓	UNHEALTHY ✗

Healthy and unhealthy food chart: Make a two column chart: one for healthy food and the other for unhealthy food. Mark underneath the title a ✓ for healthy choices and ✗ for unhealthy choices. Let children use pictures of food. Include fruits, vegetables, grains, candy, soda, etc., and allow children to place them in the right column.

Music Time

Help children learn the lyrics to sing the following song:

APPLES AND BANANAS

I like to eat, eat, eat apples and bananas
I like to eat, eat, eat apples and bananas

Now change the vowel sound to A:
I like to ate, ate, ate ay-ples and ba-nay-nays
I like to ate, ate, ate ay-ples and ba-nay-nays

Now change the vowel sound to E:
I like to eat, eat, eat ee-ples and bee-nee-nees
I like to eat, eat, eat ee-ples and bee-nee-nees

Now change the vowel sound to I:
I like to ite, ite, ite i-ples and bi-ni-nis
I like to ite, ite, ite i-ples and bi-ni-nis

Now change the vowel sound to O:
like to ote, ote, ote oh-ples and bo-no-nos
I like to ote, ote, ote oh-ples and bo-no-nos

Now change the vowel sound to U:
like to oot, oot, oot oo-ples and boo-noo-noos
I like to oot, oot, oot oo-ples and boo-noo-noos

Day #4

 **Art Activity**

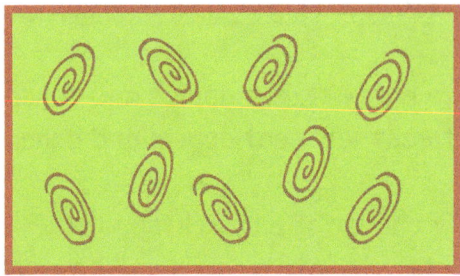

Printing beans: Provide children with green and brown paint and paper. Let children use their fingertips to print "beans."

Circle Time
Start Circle Time by gathering all children in a circle. Read <u>Lunch</u> by Denise Flemming. Ask children to list all the food the mouse ate. Ask children about a time they ate as much as the mouse in the story. Write their responses on chart paper.

Show and Tell
Ask children to bring in a poster of a nutritious recipe they made at home. The poster can include a list of the ingredients, pictures of the preparation process and the final product. Ask children to bring the lunch in to school for a tasting party.

Sensory Play
Play-dough bread: Make play-dough using any recipe. Provide children with rolling pins, plastic knives (*with adult supervision*), muffin tins, and baking trays. Allow children to roll, cut and place the dough in the muffin tins and then on the baking trays. Help children use their imagination to pretend to "bake" the dough in their play oven.

Healthy Magnetic Puzzle
Take pictures of fresh fruits and vegetables. Print doubles. Paste one set of pictures to a sheet of construction paper. Laminate. Cut out the second set of pictures and laminate them. Let children match the pictures with the ones on the construction paper.

 ### Game Play
Memory card game: Use the fruit and vegetable puzzle cards for this game activity. Ask children to sit in a circle. Place all the cards in a shoe box with a lid. Let children take the cards one by one and describe the type of food, color, etc. Then ask the children to return all the pictures to the box. Without the children noticing, hide one picture. Ask children to guess which one is missing.

 ### Math Activity

Add food stickers to wooden blocks of different sizes, making sure to assign more stickers to the larger blocks. This activity is great for sorting and number correspondence or to make patterns.

 ### Reflection
Reflecting on what children have learned about healthy and unhealthy food, can they list foods that are good for their health and growth?

Day #5

Art Activity

Dairy basket: Provide children with paper plates, paintbrushes, pipe cleaners, and pictures of dairy products. Set out trays of tempera paint of different colors. Let children paint the paper plates. Let the plates dry. Fold the paper plate in half. Glue the pictures to the paper plate. Attach a pipe cleaner from side to side to form the handle of the basket.

Circle Time

Start Circle Time by gathering all children in a circle. Read <u>The Little Red Hen</u> by Margo Zemach Sunburst. Ask children their opinion of the animals that did not help the red hen prepare the bread but wanted to be part of the feast. Write their responses on chart paper.

Science Activity

Sprouting beans: Place different types of beans in different Ziploc bags. Seal them. Let children observe the shape, size and color of the beans. Record their comments. Additionally, place lima beans in a Ziploc bag. Add a damp cotton ball inside the bag and place it next to the beans. Tape the bag to a window to get sunlight. Observe the changes and record the number of days it will take for the beans to sprout. When they are grown, you can move the seeds to the ground or small pots.

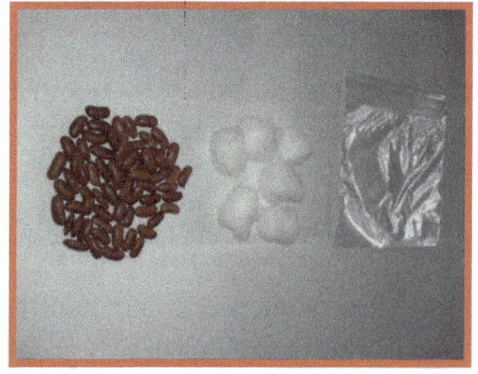

Snack Idea
Serve bread, crackers and cheese and other snacks with less fat and sugar. Include milk as a drink.

Sensory Play
Fill the sensory table with a sample of any grain group such as cereal, rice, oat and pasta. Include measuring cups, shovels, plastic spoons and sand molds. Allow children to dig, scoop out and measure the grains.

Movement
Play a music CD. When the music stops, ask children to "pop" as popcorn; "slurp" an imaginary dairy product; "swallow" meat or beans; "gulp" fruits and vegetables, etc. Then resume the music and let children dance, shake, stomp, jump or run as they wish.

Sand Play
Fill the sand table with colored rice. To do this, divide the rice in small portions and add drops of food coloring to each batch. Mix and let dry. Include a colander, different sized containers with lids, shovels, spoons and measuring cups for more fun experiences.

Writing Center
Add paper and food stickers to the writing center. Let children stick the stickers to the paper to make different designs. For more fun, add crayons and markers.

Reflection
How can children make healthier food choices despite all of the junk food TV commercials?

PLANNING WEB
Week #4

Learning Center: SOCIAL - Talk to children about the importance of using all the senses for quality life	**Learning Center: MATH** - Make sequence cards	**Learning Center: LANGUAGE/BOOKS** - <u>Wild Animals (Touch and Feel)</u> by DK Publishing	**Group Time** **Small Group:** - Noise Level Science Activity **Large Group:** - Whistle Activity Game
Learning Center: DRAMATIC PLAY - Turn the dramatic play area into a science area. Include posters of the five senses, samples of items that represent each sense such as texture props, musical toys, scented play-dough, etc.		**Developmental Goal:** - Encourage children to try things on their own - Give children opportunities to explore different activities indoors and outdoors such as puzzles, drawing, dress-up and dramatic play, art, music, science and climbing, running, etc. **Story/Theme:** - <u>The Eye Book</u> by <u>Theo LeSieg</u> **Diversity:** - Display pictures of things we can observe using all our senses	**Routines/Transitions** **Transition Chant:** Eyes are for seeing, Nose is for smelling, Tongue is for tasting, Ears are for listening but Hands are not for hitting Jacqueline Lopez
Learning Center: ART/MUSIC/MOVEMENT - Feely painting - Noise makers - Rhyme, "Open, Shut Them." - Scented Paint	**INDOORS OUTDOORS** <u>Indoors</u>: - Make a texture book <u>Outdoors</u>: - Bumpy floor game	**Health/Nutrition/Cooking** <u>Snack Idea</u>: - Serve a crunchy snack	**Learning Center: SCIENCE/SENSORY** - Fill trays with cold, room temperature and lukewarm water - Make slime

CLASS GOAL

Week #4

THE FIVE SENSES

Day #1

Art Activity

Feely Painting: Set up the art table with paper, finger-paint, salt, and spoons. Let children add a spoon of salt to a dab of paint on the paper. Allow children to spread the paint on the paper using their hands.

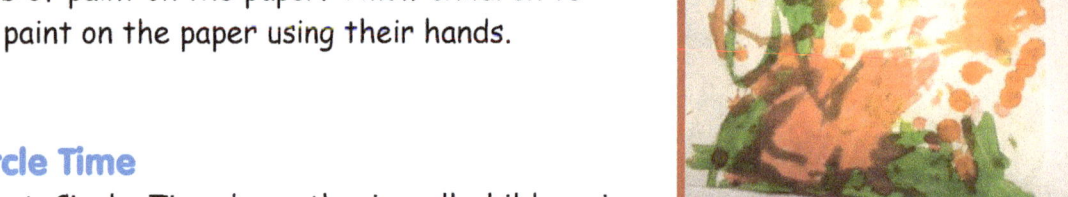

Circle Time

Start Circle Time by gathering all children in a circle. Read <u>Wild Animals (Touch and Feel)</u> by DK Publishing. Ask children to describe how it feels to touch the rough lizard, the sticky tree frog or the furry lion. Write their responses on chart paper.

Sensory Play

Feely Box: Place several plastic toys inside the feely box. Have each child reach in the box and pull out an object. Ask children to feel, touch and name the object before pulling it out.

Science Activity

Set up the science table with three aluminum trays. Fill the first tray with cold water and ice cubes. Ask children to describe how it feels. Fill the second tray with room temperature water. Again, ask children to describe how it feels. Finally, fill the last tray with lukewarm water. Ask children to put their hands in and describe what they feel. Record theirs answers.

Writing Center

Texture Book: Provide children with sheets of construction paper, glue and different items for children to feel and touch. Include feathers, fabric paper, collage material such as pom-poms, crepe paper, yarn, corrugated paper, etc. Have children describe how the items feel as they put together their texture book.

Game Play

Bumpy floor: Prepare a bumpy floor. Find an empty carpet area. Gather different items such as egg cartons, wrapping paper, and empty toilet paper tubes. Remove the lids from the egg cartons. Tape the egg carton to the carpet leaving the bumpy side up. Arrange the toilet tubes around the egg cartons and tape them. Cut squares of bubble wrap paper and tape it next to the egg cartons. Ask children to take their shoes off and walk across the bumpy surface.

Science Activity

Make Slime: Gather school glue, water, food coloring, and borax. Mix ½ cup of Elmer's glue and two or three drops of food coloring with ½ cup of water. Mix well. Dissolve 1 tsp. of borax in 1 cup of water. Mix well. Pour slowly the borax solution into the glue solution stirring constantly. Store the solution in a tight container in the refrigerator.

Puzzle

Provide children with puzzles they know well with not too many pieces. Dump the pieces on the table and ask children to put the pieces back together.

Reflection

Which part of the body is responsible for the sense of touch?
What do we use our senses for?

Day #2

Art Activity

Free Painting: Set up the art table with different collage materials, paper, finger-paints, tempera paints, dot paints, brushes, glue, etc. Let children see and decide what types of materials they would like to use for their project.

Circle Time

Start Circle Time by gathering all children in a circle. Read <u>The Eye Book</u> by <u>Theo LeSieg</u>. Ask children to list all the things they can see with their eyes. What are some of the things the boy and the rabbit could see looking down holes? Write their responses on chart paper.

Math Activity

Sequence cards: Cut out pictures from magazines. Glue each picture to an index card. Cut in half. Laminate. Mix up the picture halves and place them face up on the table. Let children pick a card and find the matching half from the pile.

Field Trip

Nature Walk: Take children for a nature walk or to the playground. Ask children to observe what they see. Stop for children to point out interesting sights. Encourage them to use descriptive words to explain what they see.

Show and Tell

Ask children to bring any item from home for Show and Tell. Allow time for children to describe the shape, color, use, etc., of the item.

Water Play

Fill the water table. Similar to I Spy, describe an item children can bring to the water table. Let children guess and look for the object.

Finger Play

Help children sing and act out the following rhyme:

OPEN, SHUT THEM
Sung to "Open, Shut Them"

Open, shut them,
Open, shut them,
Give a little wink, wink, wink.
Roll them, squint them,
Roll them, squint them,
But don't let them stare at you!

Jacqueline Lopez

Game Play

Set up an obstacle course. Use balance beams, hula-hoops, traffic cones, play tunnels, etc. Mark one end as the start and the other end as the finish. Encourage children to twist, jump, hop, climb, or crawl to get to the finish line.

Writing Center

Set up the writing center with paints of different colors, markers, crayons, stickers, glue, collage materials, etc. Give each child two toilet paper tubes and let children decorate the tubes with the colors and designs of their choice. Cut a little strip of Velcro to attach the two tubes. Punch holes on the outside of each cardboard tube and tie some yarn to hang the binoculars from the neck.

Reflection

What are some things you can see?
How could you describe an object if you couldn't see it?

Day #3

Art Activity

Rice Shaker Tambourine: Provide children with paper plates, paints of different colors, paintbrushes, strips of crepe paper, tape, glue, stickers, rice or lentils. First, allow children to decorate their paper plates (two per child) as they wish. Then pour rice or lentils in the middle of the plate. Glue the plates together and additionally, secure them with tape. Let children paste the strips of crepe paper to give the tambourines a little flair. Give the tambourines to the children to shake as they dance.

Circle Time

Start Circle Time by gathering all children in a circle. Read Noisy Barn: With Four Farm Sounds by Roger Priddy. Ask children to list all the things they can hear with their ears. What kinds of noises can children imitate? Write their responses on chart paper.

Movement

Record familiar sounds children will able to recognize such as the sound of clapping hands, running water, a chugging train, a police siren, and sounds of farm animals. Let the children listen to the sounds and name them.

Snack Idea

Crunchy snack: Serve a crunchy snack such as crackers, carrot sticks, apple slices or cereal.

Game Play

Whistle Activity Game: Sit children in a circle to explain the rules of the game. Inform children that they are going to participate in a whistle game. When children hear the whistle, they will have to move according to the times it is blown. For example, one whistle, one step forward; two whistles, two jumps; three whistles, three somersaults; four whistles, four steps backwards; five whistles, five twists, etc. The winner will blow the whistle for the next run.

One Whistle	1 Step Forward
Two Whistles	2 Jumps
Three Whistles	3 Somersaults
Four Whistles	4 Steps Backwards
Five Whistles	5 Twists

Science Activity

Noise Level: Prepare this activity ahead of time. Gather plastic containers of all sizes, plastic bottles, glue, rice, beans, sand, pebbles, and coins. Fill each container with different items. Let each child pick one container and listen closely to the sound it makes by shaking the container near the ear. Compare the sounds that each shaker makes. Record the results.

Writing Center

Noise Book: Set up the writing area with paper, glue, old magazines, and scissors. Help children tear or cut pictures of things that make sounds and glue them to the paper. Punch several holes on the pages and string a piece of yarn to make a book.

Game Play

Playing drums: Set out cans of different sizes. Provide children with wooden beads, beans, rice, lentils, etc. Ask children to drop any of these items inside the cans. Make sure to fill no more than a quarter of the can. Cover the can and secure the can with tape. Encourage children to play drums on the can.

Day #4

Art Activity

<u>Scented Paint:</u> Provide children with glue, powdered tempera, Kool-Aid powder, and foam meat trays. Let children squeeze the glue on the trays to make a design. Mix ¾ cup of powdered tempera with ¼ cup of Kool-Aid. Sprinkle this mixture on top and let dry. Shake off loose powder when dry.

Circle Time

Start Circle Time by gathering all children in a circle. Read <u>David Smells! A Diaper David Book</u> by David Shannon. Ask children to describe their favorite part of the story. Ask them to name other things David did that showed the use of all his senses such as petting the dog or banging on a drum. Write their responses on chart paper.

Water Play

Add vanilla extract and food coloring to the water table. Include measuring cups and plastic containers of different sizes.

Science Activity

<u>Smelling Test:</u> You will need cotton balls, onions, food extract, perfume, cinnamon sticks, vinegar, etc. Dip the cotton balls in the vanilla extract, vinegar, and perfume. Allow children to sniff the scents of the cotton balls and the other foods.

Math Activity

<u>Smell Chart:</u> Ask children to bring in fruits or vegetables that have strong smells. Place all the items in a bag. One at a time, blindfold each child or ask the child to close his/her eyes and pick one item from the bag. Encourage the child to sniff and identify the item from the bag.

Sensory Play

Scented Play-dough: Make play-dough. Divide the dough into three batches and add drops of food extract such as vanilla, peppermint, orange, and lemon to each batch. Provide children with play-dough tools and the scented dough. If desirable, add food coloring.

Music Time

Ask children to sing and act out the following song:

THE MULBERRY BUSH
Sung to: "The Mulberry Bush"

Here we go 'round the mulberry bush,
The mulberry bush, the mulberry bush.
Here we go 'round the mulberry bush,
So early in the morning.

This is the way we sniff our food,
Sniff our food, sniff our food
This is the way we sniff our food,
So early in the morning.

This is the way we smell a flower,
Smell a flower, smell a flower,
This is the way we smell a flower,
So early in the morning.

Jacqueline Lopez

Substitute *sniff our food* for *whiff the air*, etc.

Day #5

 **Art Activity**

Edible Painting: Provide children with plain yogurt, food coloring, large chunks of marshmallows, cinnamon sticks and food foam trays. Make three paint trays (or more) by mixing the yogurt with different food coloring. Mix well. Spread the mixture on the trays using the marshmallows or cinnamon sticks as paintbrushes.

Circle Time
Start Circle Time by gathering all children in a circle. Read <u>My Five Senses</u> by Margaret Miller. Ask children to describe their favorite part of the story or describe what they see, hear, smell, touch or hear in the classroom. Write their responses on chart paper.

 Math Activity
Sweet and Sour: Provide children with a variety of food for them to taste. Classify the food as sweet, sour, salty or bitter. Record the results.

TYPE OF FOOD	SWEET	SOUR	SALTY	BITTER

Writing Center

Paper Plate Food: Provide children with food stickers, grocery food magazines, paper and glue. Let children glue the pictures of their favorite food or attach the stickers to the paper. When they have finished, encourage children to share what their favorite food is and to describe its taste.

Snack Idea

Edible Necklace: Provide children with cheerios, marshmallows and string. For each necklace, string a pattern of cereal and marshmallows. Tie ends together using a double knot to make a necklace.

Science Activity

Mix and Taste Activity Game: Provide children with paper bowls, crackers, jelly, cream cheese, and butter. Divide the crackers into three bowls. Spread the crackers with the jelly, cream cheese and butter. Let children taste the three different flavored crackers. Make a chart of the children's favorite cracker.

Dramatic Play

Turn the dramatic play area into a science area. Include posters of the five senses, books, samples of items that represent each sense such as texture props, musical toys, scented play-dough, a box with things children can sort and classify, pictures of food, etc.

Reflection

Encourage children to pay close attention to the things that they see, hear, smell, taste and feel.
Reflecting on what children learned, how can using our five senses help us in our daily lives?

HELPFUL RESOURCES / LINKS

NATIONAL:

The National Association for the Education of Young Children (NAEYC)
www.naeyc.org

The National Early Childhood Technical Assistance Center (NECTAC)
Early Learning Guidelines/Early Childhood Standards
http://www.nectac.org/topics/quality/earlylearn.asp

The Early Childhood Outcomes Center (ECO Center)
http://projects.fpg.unc.edu/~eco/index.cfm

Research and Training Center on Early Childhood Development
http://www.researchtopractice.info/index.php

Teaching Our Youngest: A Guide for Preschool Teachers and Child Care and Family Providers
U.S. Department of Education
http://www2.ed.gov/teachers/how/early/teachingouryoungest/index.html

CONNECTICUT:

Connecticut's Guidelines for the Development of Infant & Toddler Early Learning
A Handbook for Caregivers of Young Children
Developed by the Connecticut Department of Social Services

Connecticut State Department of Education
Early Childhood Education
http://www.sde.ct.gov/sde/cwp/view.asp?a=2678&Q=320780

Connecticut State Department of Education
Performance Standards and Description of Benchmarks for 2 ½ to 6 Year-Old-Children
http://www.sde.ct.gov/sde/lib/sde/PDF/DEPS/Early/Preschool_framework.pdf

The State Department of Education's document Connecticut Preschool Assessment Framework (2008) can be accessed at:
http://www.sde.ct.gov/sde/lib/sde/PDF/DEPS/Early/Preschool_Assessment_Framework.pdf
along with the accompanying flipchart at:
http://www.sde.ct.gov/sde/lib/sde/pdf/deps/early/flipchart.pdf

State Education Resource Center (SERC)
http://ctserc.org/s/
Information on professional development, latest research and best practices to educators, service providers, and families throughout the state

RHODE ISLAND:
Ready to Learn Providence
945 Westminster Street
Providence, Rhode island 02903
www.r2lp.org

About the Author
JACQUELINE SALAZAR DE LÓPEZ

Jacqueline Salazar De López is a preschool teacher in the state of Connecticut with almost two decades of experience working with toddlers and two-year-olds. Over the years, she has facilitated workshops in early childhood education. Jacqueline is also a curriculum consultant at Our Lady of Grace Preschool & Kindergarten in Stamford. She obtained a Child Development Associate (CDA) from Norwalk Community College and is currently pursuing a Masters in Education at Manhattanville College.

In her book, Jacqueline helps teachers engage in developmentally appropriate practice, creating daily routines and meaningful experiences that respond individually to children's strengths, interests, and needs. Jacqueline shares her years of experience as an educator with other teachers, caregivers and parents. A mother of three children, Jacqueline worked alongside her husband and her mother to develop the art activities featured in the book.

www.ingramcontent.com/pod-product-compliance
Lightning Source LLC
Chambersburg PA
CBHW081825300426
44116CB00014B/2483